MARTYRDOM:
THE FINAL TRIUMPH
OF FAITH

This textbook was written by members of the faculty and staff of Bob Jones University. Standing for the "old-time religion" and the absolute authority of the Bible since 1927, Bob Jones University is the world's leading Fundamentalist Christian university. The staff of the University is devoted to educating Christian men and women to be servants of Jesus Christ in all walks of life.

Providing unparalleled academic excellence, Bob Jones University prepares its students through its offering of over one hundred majors, while its fervent spiritual emphasis prepares their minds and hearts for service and devotion to the Lord Jesus Christ.

If you would like more information about the spiritual and academic opportunities available at Bob Jones University, please call

1-800-BJ-AND-ME (1-800-252-6363).
www.bju.edu

NOTE:

The fact that materials produced by other publishers may be referred to in this volume does not constitute an endorsement by Bob Jones University Press of the content or theological position of materials produced by such publishers. The position of Bob Jones University Press, and the University itself, is well known. Any references and ancillary materials are listed as an aid to the student or the teacher and in an attempt to maintain the accepted academic standards of the publishing industry.

Martyrdom: The Final Triumph of Faith

Scott Anderson, M.A.
Daniel Cruver, M.S.

Editor: Thomas Parr
Designer: Noelle Snyder
Cover designer: John Bjerk
Composition: Rebecca G. Zollinger and Agnieszka Augustyniak

CONTENTS

Introduction

Those people are "impossible to tame. They attack any civilized person who comes near them." They "slip up and club their victims in their hammocks. You'll never come back alive." Imagine remaining steadfast in your decision to take the gospel to an uncivilized tribe when people confronted you with a warning such as this. Would you back out of your commitment to bring them the gospel of Christ?

Cecil and Dorothy Dye and their three children, along with six other adults, refused to allow terrifying reports to deter them from following the Lord's will. In 1946, Cecil and Dorothy led this group to take the gospel to the Ayores, an Indian tribe in Bolivia. They moved to the heart of the jungle of Santo Corazon where the Ayores lived.

It was from this campsite in Santo Corazon on November 10, 1946 that five men, including Cecil, planned to make their first contact with the Indians. Not many days after their first hike they encountered an Ayore who was tending his crops. He saw the approaching men, who were extending gifts of knives, machetes, and clothing, and immediately ran to his village yelling about civilized men approaching. Everyone in the Ayore village went into hiding, armed with primitive weapons.

The five missionaries slowly walked into the midst of the village, holding out their gifts, hoping to demonstrate their good intentions. An Ayore shot an arrow at one of the men and hit him in the shoulder. One of the other men immediately pulled it out of his shoulder. Dropping some of the gifts, they began to walk out of the village as quickly as they could. The Indians ran to seize the gifts left by the missionaries. One Indian named Upoide, upset that he still lacked a machete, angrily went after the men to get one.

When Upoide caught up with the missionaries, they offered more machetes and knives and made friendly gestures to him. He approached Dave Bacon, the smallest of the men, and extended his arms, wanting the machete that Dave was holding. Dave gave him the machete. Upoide then stepped back and plunged his spear into Dave's body. Another Ayore arrived on the scene and ended Dave's life with a blow to the head. Fearing that the remaining missionaries would retaliate because of the death of their friend, other Ayores attacked them with spears and clubs. Not one of the five men survived the brutal attack. However, the Lord used this event to make the Indians receptive to the gospel. Later, some were saved and told of what happened.[1]

Surprised by Suffering?

Should we be surprised when God-honoring missionaries or pastors are persecuted and even martyred while doing the will of God? Should our first response to stories of persecution be, "We cannot believe this is happening!"? With reference to the believer's response to suffering, Peter states, "Beloved, think it not strange [do not be surprised] concerning the fiery trial which is to try you, as though some strange thing happened unto you: But rejoice, inasmuch as ye are partakers of Christ's sufferings" (I Pet. 4:12-13a). It is clear that believers should not be surprised by suffering.

Should we be concerned when Christians are facing very little if any persecution for their faith in Christ?

Obviously, this is not the right question for us to be asking. Perhaps the question that needs to be asked is this: "Should we be concerned when Christians are facing very little if any persecution for their faith in Christ?" Yes, we should be concerned when the absence of Christian persecution is due to a preoccupation with earthly pursuits and comforts. It is clear in Scripture that Christians are not to be preoccupied with the things of this world

(Luke 12:15-34). By persecution we are referring to trials (some form of ridicule, rejection, or loss) that are experienced by those who live godly in this

There is a godliness that invokes persecution.

world. If we don't experience trials because we seek after what the world seeks after (Luke 12:29-31), or because we choose the comfortable path of least resistance in this world, then we should be greatly concerned.

What Do You Do with This Verse?

Consider what Paul says in II Timothy 3:12: "Yea, and all that will live godly in Christ Jesus shall suffer persecution." Notice that Paul explicitly states that those whose lives are characterized by a purposeful choice to live godly will be persecuted. Paul leaves no room for doubt as to whether or not persecution will come. So what are Christians who do not experience any form of persecution to do with this verse?

A pastor from Holland tells of his experience with this

lifestyle-challenging verse. He was visiting a group of pastors in Budapest, Hungary. One afternoon they were all sitting together in a room listening to him speak. Midway through the meeting, a pastor from Romania who just recently had been released from prison walked into the room. The room turned silent out of respect for this man who had suffered dearly for his faith in Christ. After a few moments of silence, this Romanian pastor began to speak to the pastor from Holland. "Are there any pastors in prison in Holland?" "No," the pastor answered. The Romanian pastor inquired as to why this was the case. The pastor from Holland thoughtfully answered, "I think it must be because we do not take advantage of all the opportunities God gives us." Not being satisfied with the answer, the Romanian said, "What do you do with II Timothy 3:12?" The pastor from Holland turned to the verse and read it. After a moment he answered, "Brother, please forgive me. We do nothing with that verse."[2]

How would you have answered this Romanian pastor? The point is not that if Christians do not find themselves in prison from time to time, they are not living godly. The point is that we should live in such a way that if our political or cultural climate became like Romania's was, we would find ourselves in danger of being cast into prison. You see, II Timothy 3:12 is a verse that we must come to grips with if our lives are to please God. Paul reveals that there is a godliness that invokes persecution. It is a godliness that is lived "in Christ Jesus." But what does a life lived this way look like? Are we living the kind of godly life that Paul speaks of here? In order to answer this question, we must examine the context of this passage. Paul's statement in verse 12 concerning persecution follows a reference to some persecutions out of which the Lord delivered him (3:11). Paul specifically refers to persecutions that he faced at Antioch, Iconium, and Lystra. What did Paul do or say that invoked persecution?

Acts 13:44-50 tells us that persecution came upon Paul in Antioch because he was preaching the Word of God. Acts 14:1-5 tells us that in Iconium persecution came upon Paul because he was testifying of God's grace. In Lystra persecution also came upon him because of his preaching. Jews from Antioch and Iconium had followed Paul to Lystra, stoned him, and left him for dead (Acts 14:19-20). So what exactly does persecution-invoking godliness look like? In Paul's life this godliness manifested itself with bold words of truth for God. For Paul, living godly meant being a

witness to those who did not know Christ.

Godliness: What Grace Expects

Titus 2:11-12 states that "the grace of God that bringeth salvation hath appeared to all men, teaching us that, denying ungodliness and worldly lusts, we should live soberly, righteously, and *godly,* in this present world." The godliness that grace teaches us to live is the godliness of II Timothy 3:12 that invokes persecution. Paul was persecuted in Antioch, Iconium, and Lystra because he was a student of grace, the great educator of godly living. Titus 2:11-12 teaches us that saving grace ever teaches those who are believing in Christ to live this persecution-invoking, godly life.

If saving grace teaches believers that those whom it saves must live godly, and Scripture teaches that those who live godly in Christ Jesus shall suffer persecution, then we should not at all be surprised when Christians around the world suffer for the cause of Christ. But we should be concerned enough when Christians do not experience some form or persecution to determine why they do not. The persecution and martyrdom of Christians is a testimony to the irrefutable fact that grace is on the move in the world. Scripture gives us no grounds for being surprised that believers are persecuted and martyred. But we do have grounds for concern if we do not experience some form of persecution. If we live godly in Christ Jesus, persecution is to be expected.

---

*Throughout this book italics are used in Scripture passages for emphasis.

Does God ordain that some of His children suffer martyrdom? Consider the following verse, which speaks of future martyred saints; note especially the words in italics.

"White robes were given unto every one of them; and it was said unto them, that they should rest yet for a little season, until their fellowservants also and their brethren, that *should be killed* as they were, *should be fulfilled*" (Rev. 6:11).

The Goal of This Book

This book is not calling you to actively seek martyrdom or persecution. Rather, it is exhorting you to live a radically God-centered life, to actively live godly in Christ Jesus, realizing that often in the providence of God those who live godly in Christ Jesus are martyred. It is not a choice that believers make for themselves. If a believer dies a martyr's death, it is because it was ordained by God (Rev. 6:11).

The title of our book, *Martyrdom: The Final Triumph of Faith,* implies that there are many triumphs of faith in God-centered living. A Christian's life is a journey in which he triumphs by faith over many dangers, toils, and snares. And for some believers, this journey ends in martyrdom. The saving grace of God starts every believer on this journey so that he participates in faith's many triumphs along the way. So the question for you is not, "Will you give yourself to be a martyr?" but "Will you give yourself to radical God-centered living and leave the outcome of your life in God's omnipotent hands?" The aim of this book is to increase your faith so that you will daily give yourself to passionate, God-centered living regardless of the cost.

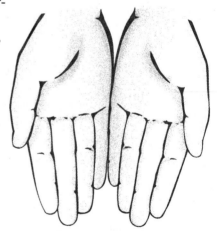

What You Will Need

If you really desire to benefit spiritually from this book, you must read it with an open Bible. We have attempted to deeply root everything in the text of Scripture. It is

The persecution and martyrdom of Christians is a testimony to the irrefutable fact that grace is on the move in the world.

up to you to examine whether or not the things we write find their basis in the Word of God. This was the practice of the first century Berean believers as they received teaching from the Apostle Paul (Acts 17:10-11). This book should drive you to the Scriptures as you seek to live godly in this present world. As you read, follow along in your own Bible. This book is only as beneficial as it accurately represents the teaching of the Scriptures. May the Word of God be your discerning guide as you read.

CHAPTER ONE

Does a Martyr Ever Die Alone?

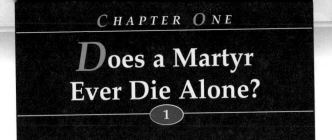

Left Alone

When it comes down to it, who really wants to die alone, separated from friends and family, especially if it is a terrifying and painful death? In 1951, a bachelor named Dave Yarwood joined several other missionaries who were already in South America to reach the Nhambiquaras Indians with the gospel of Jesus Christ. Dave was very eager to make contact with these rarely seen, uncivilized Indians. After repeated trips deep into the jungle from their base camp over a period of months, Dave and his companions were still no closer to making contact. They had not seen a single Indian. But unknown to them, contact was to be made when it was not expected.

One hot August day the men ventured down a river away from their camp to gather turtle eggs for food. (Turtle eggs were the closest thing they could find to chicken eggs.) They decided to beach their canoe on a large sandbar and begin hunting for eggs. The men spread out to cover more ground, and it was not too long before Dave unexpectedly found what was unmistakably an Indian's footprint.

Immediately the turtle egg hunt turned into a search for Nhambiquaras Indians. Just a few days later the long-awaited first contact was made. The

When it comes down to it, who really wants to die alone?

missionaries happened upon four Indian men. From that point on, the missionaries actively sought to develop peaceful relations with the Indians through the giving of gifts. Progress was made, but it was slow. The Indians could be rough at times, unexpectedly forcing their fingers into the missionaries' mouths to search them or grabbing a missionary around the neck and almost choking the life out of him for fun.

Several days into one of their extended stays near the Indians' camp, the missionaries decided it was time to return to their base camp for a week or two to gather more supplies. They assumed that all of the men would go together until Dave Yarwood insisted that he stay behind to continue interacting with their new friends. He did not wish to lose any of the momentum that they had gained. Dave's companions were entirely against it. But Dave was a large and determined man, and his determination finally won out. They begrudgingly agreed that they would let big Dave stay behind to continue befriending the Indians.

Several days after his companions left, Dave was preparing to eat a can of Spam when he heard a signal from the Indians for him to cross the river. This was the usual way that the Indians informed the missionaries that they wanted to meet with them. Dave jumped into his canoe and crossed the river. As he got out of his canoe and began walking to the usual meeting place, two arrows came jetting out of the woods and pierced his chest. Dave stumbled and turned and, as best as he could, began to run back to his canoe to escape his attackers. As he ran, two more arrows penetrated his back. Left alone in the jungle, Dave died shortly thereafter. Dave Yarwood died alone in the deep jungle far from friends and loved ones. When Dave's companions returned and found his decaying body, their broken hearts ached with the thought that their dear friend died alone in his service for Christ.[3]

The Motivating Cloud of Witnesses

Did Dave Yarwood *really* die a martyr's death alone? In answering our question, we must consider Hebrews 12:1, which says, "Wherefore seeing we also are compassed about with so great a cloud of witnesses, let us lay aside every weight, and the sin which doth so easily beset us, and let us run with patience the race that is set before us."

The main point in this verse is the command to "run with patience." Everything else in the verse is in some way subordinate to this command. The first part of the verse gives us a motivation for running and finishing the race we are to run. Some believers end the race dying of natural causes; others are martyred. But whether we ultimately die of natural causes or are martyred alone in the jungle, the motivation still applies. If we put the motivation and the command together in a single thought, here is what we have: since "we also are compassed about [surrounded] with so great a cloud of witnesses . . . let us run!"

There are two questions that we need to answer in order to understand properly the significance of this main thought. (1) Who are these witnesses that surround us? (2) How do they motivate us to run and finish the race that is set before us?

Who Are These Witnesses?

The answer to this question is found in the very first word of Hebrews 12:1, *wherefore*. This word is critically important. It connects chapter 12 with chapter 11. It essentially tells us that we cannot let chapter 12 stand in isolation from what precedes it. We cannot properly interpret Hebrews 12:1 without chapter 11. So what necessary information do we find in Hebrews 11?

Key Interpretive Questions

1. Who are these witnesses?
2. How do they motivate us?

Chapter 12 is preceded by a record of Old Testament men and women who fought the fight of faith and won.

Many of these witnesses of Hebrews 11, being thrown into the volcanic rage of the world, were persecuted and martyred for their faith in Christ. Some were put on trial where they were cruelly mocked and scourged (11:36). Others were stoned or sawn in two (11:37*a*). Some escaped death only to wander about from place to place, wearing garments of the poorest condition (11:37*b*). These all finished the same race that we are running, and they finished victoriously. So the witnesses of Hebrews 12:1 are the courageous men and women of Hebrews 11.

How Do They Motivate Us?

How were these witnesses to motivate Dave Yarwood as he sought to live a radically God-centered life by taking the gospel to an uncivilized people—and for that matter, how should these witnesses motivate us? The word *witness* can refer to one who saw an event take place or to one who testifies to others of what he knows. The Greek word for *witness* is *martureo,* from which we get our English word *martyr.* So first we see that the witnesses of Hebrews 11 are martyrs. Martyrs are witnesses. But in what sense are they witnesses? Are they merely those who saw an event take place, or are they those who are testifying of what they know?

Since all the witnesses of Hebrews 11 have been dead for a few millennia, can they still testify of what they know to be true? Yes, they can and do. Consider what Scripture states about one of the witnesses of Hebrews 11 who was murdered. Verse 4 states that Abel though "being dead yet speaketh." Death did not silence

Abel's voice. The text clearly states that he is yet speaking or testifying though he is no longer on earth. This gives us a textual basis for concluding that the witnesses of Hebrews 11 still testify of what

Believers who have finished the race confirm that God is a great rewarder (Heb. 11:6) of those who live and die in faith.

they know. So of what do the witnesses of Hebrews 11 testify? By God's design, believers who have finished the race confirm that God is a great rewarder (Heb. 11:6) of those who live and die in faith.

So how did they motivate Dave Yarwood, and how do they motivate us? As we consider the Scripture's account of their finishing the same race we run, their lives declare to us the reality of the future joy (Heb. 13:7). In essence, through their living and dying they say to us, "We finished the race in victory and so can you!"

Did Dave Yarwood Die Alone?

Christians who live and die in service to Christ never live and die alone. God has given us abundant confirming testimony for our comfort and encouragement. The Scriptures teach that if we wish to live and die well, we must live and die with the confirming testimonies of Abel, Abraham, Moses, and others ringing in our hearts. Which is better—to die in the company of loved ones without any confirming testimony of what lies beyond death, or to die separated from all friends and loved ones yet surrounded by sure testimonies of future joy?

Alone but Not Alone

There is another witness from the past whose life encourages us to believe that martyrs never die alone. The martyrdom of New Testament saints began with the brutal death of Stephen. As a young man Stephen stood alone in the face of his bloodthirsty

Have you ever noticed that every action attributed to the men and women of Hebrews 11 is said to have been done either *through* or *by faith*. As we run the race set before us, how important is faith in God and in His Word?

persecutors. What if he did not have the great benefit of knowing the testimonies of Hebrews 11? Would Stephen have been left to face suffering and death with nothing but his own thoughts and fears? What is it that strengthened Stephen in those last moments of his life?

We meet Stephen for the first time in Acts 6:5 where he is described as "a man full of faith." The Book of Acts devotes seventy-three verses (6:5–8:2) to Stephen, mainly accounting for his preaching and martyr's death. Yet the first thing said of Stephen is not that he was a martyr but that he was blessed with abundant faith. This clearly places him in the company of witnesses found in Hebrews 11. Now why is this the first thing said about him?

Twice in Acts' account of Stephen, we have reference to Saul of Tarsus. The Holy Spirit considered it important enough to record that Stephen's executioners laid their garments at Saul's feet. Saul was a consenting participant at Stephen's stoning, and as a result he witnessed firsthand Stephen's shining testimony of Christ. So why did the Holy Spirit see fit to include this *minor* detail in this account? One truth we can learn from the details of this account is that the blood of the martyrs is the seed of the church. Out of the blood of Stephen came Paul, the bold apostle to the Gentiles.

Acts first describes him as "a man full of faith" so that we see everything Stephen said and did in relationship to his faith. Everything recorded concerning what Stephen said and did reveals a man who by faith had an inextinguishable passion for Jesus, his Lord. Stephen's passion was made manifest by his boldness to speak the truth concerning Jesus (6:9–7:53), knowing full well that it might cost him his life (7:54–8:2).

The Connecting Link

So what is the connection between Stephen's being "a man full of faith" and his boldness to speak the truth concerning Jesus in the face of almost certain death? Through faith in the Scriptures, Stephen was able to see something that held great power over him, some-

thing beyond the ugly threat of death. Through faith Stephen saw death, not as a trap door opening into a dark abyss, but as a palace door opening into the very throne room of God.

Faith in God is what enables a believer to die "alone" as a martyr if need be. The reason someone can experience this kind of enabling faith is that its object is none other than the God of the universe. By faith in what God revealed in the Scriptures, Stephen saw death, not as his mortal enemy, but as his God-ordained servant leading him to heaven's throne room.

Through faith Stephen saw death, not as a trap door opening into a dark abyss, but as a palace door opening into the very throne room of God.

Stephen's death in the infancy of the church was the beginning of a long and glorious tribute to the triumph of faith in martyrdom. Stephen, like the men and women of Hebrews 11, lived the life of faith. Through the eyes of faith, they saw the unseen, eternal realities (II Cor. 4:16-18), which radically altered the way they viewed the visible, temporal world that surrounded them. Although there were no fellow believers suffering the same fate by Stephen's side, he faced his executioners with courage, knowing the eternal realities that he would soon personally experience. His thoughts were not on what he was losing, but on what he was gaining (Acts 7:56).

God Never Leaves His Children Alone.

In Hebrews 13:5, the Lord promises, "I will never leave thee, nor forsake thee." Christian martyrs never die alone. God has made ample provisions so that his people can face a martyr's death with hope and courage, knowing that they will not be left alone in those hugely significant final moments. God has provided us with the confirming testimony of those who have gone on before and the ability to see the unseen world through the eyes of faith. What kind of confidence should this give you to live a passionately God-centered life, a life of active godliness? What is there for us to fear? Could you be another Dave Yarwood? Or rather, are you being another Dave Yarwood, living a life of active godliness in Christ Jesus?

A Prayer of Response

Father, the testimony of Stephen and of Dave Yarwood has sobered me to realize that I need to be living for the kingdom of God's unseen realities. The journey of faith is a life-dominating journey that may end in blood, sweat, and tears. I pray, Father, that I, like Stephen, may see life through the eyes of faith; that I would be found faithful unto death, knowing that Jesus is Lord of heaven and earth. To our great Savior belongs all power and authority. Purge me of any phoniness and insincerity, that I may be, as Stephen was, described as one "full of faith." In Jesus' name I pray, Amen.

CHAPTER TWO

The Blood of the Martyrs

2

"The Church of Christ has been founded by shedding its own blood, not that of others; by enduring outrage, not inflicting it. Persecutions have made it grow; martyrdoms have crowned it."—Jerome, Letter 82

Persecution Through the Centuries

What began as a trickle in the days of Stephen and the apostles soon became a raging river of global persecution intent on sweeping the church out of existence. In the early years, the threat was primarily Jewish. But within a generation the wrath of the mighty Roman Empire was unleashed in fury. For nearly 250 years, under the direction of ten different Roman emperors, believers faced unprecedented persecution. Tens of thousands of Christians were martyred in the arenas of Rome for the entertainment of the masses.

And though there were intermittent periods of rest for the church, the pages of history reveal continual persecutions of those who held fast to the gospel. During the Middle Ages it took the form of the Catholic Church's Inquisition. Often it was the mandate of great European monarchs. Missionaries of the 1800s felt it from the very people they were trying to reach. Indeed, the flood of persecution against believers has continued right up to our present day. In fact, it is estimated that more Christians were martyred in the twentieth century than in all the preceding centuries combined.

How Did They Die?
The Martyrdom of Jesus' Disciples
(according to tradition)

"And ye shall be hated of all men for my name's sake. . . ."—Mark 13:13

Peter—crucified head downward

James—executed with the sword

John—survived being placed in a cauldron of boiling oil; banished to the Isle of Patmos

Andrew—crucified

Philip—tied to a pillar and stoned

Bartholomew (Nathanael)—flayed alive and beheaded

Matthew—nailed to the ground and beheaded

Thomas—burnt alive in a furnace and speared to death

James, son of Alphaeus—thrown off the pinnacle of the Temple, stoned, and finally beaten to death with a club

Simon Zelotes—crucified

Judas (Thaddaeus)—beaten to death with rods

Portraits of Martyrs

To help better understand the price that has been paid for the sake of Christ, this chapter contains cameo portraits of several famous (and some not so famous) Christian martyrs. The purpose of this chapter is to give you a broader perspective of the suffering believers have endured through the centuries and to encourage you with a great cloud of martyred witnesses that have gone before. In spite of every attempt of wicked men to stop the spread of the work of Christ, the gospel has triumphed. Yes, Tertullian was right; the blood of the martyrs is the seed of the church. The more believers suffer well for the sake of Christ and the gospel, the more the church grows.

"We [Christians] multiply when we are mown down by you; the blood of Christians is seed. Dying we conquer. The moment we are crushed, that moment we go forth victorious."—Tertullian, Apologeticus 50

Read these pages slowly, thoughtfully, reverently. Allow yourself to enter into these martyrs' circumstances. Note their passion for God and His glory. Feel the beat of the martyrs' hearts. And let your own heart be moved by these men and women whose faith in the gospel stood firm until the end.

Ignatius

One of the earliest and most notable Christian martyrs was Ignatius, the leader of the church at Antioch in Syria. Tradition holds that he may have been discipled by the apostle John. Ignatius was well known for his love for God and faithful testimony of Christ. He would often say, "The crucified Christ is my only and entire love."

It was in the twelfth year of the reign of Emperor Trajan that the Roman armies won several decisive military victories. While in Antioch, the Emperor decided to give credit to the Roman gods for these military successes. On one of these occasions, Ignatius, a bold preacher of righteousness, openly reproved the Emperor for his pagan idolatry. Emperor Trajan was infuriated and immediately seized Ignatius and had him transported to Rome for punishment. While in transport, Ignatius's sentence was made known: he was to be torn to pieces by wild beasts in the arena at Rome.

"The crucified Christ is my only and entire love."

On his way there, Ignatius wrote several pastoral letters to the churches of Asia Minor. Many of these letters still exist today. Each is filled with wisdom, warning, and tender greetings. From these letters it becomes apparent that Ignatius was not dreading the fate that awaited him in Rome but rather looked forward to the privilege of suffering for Christ's sake. In one letter Ignatius states, "Let the devil and evil men afflict me with all manner of pain

and torment, with fire, with cross, with fighting against wild beasts, with scattering of the members and bones of my body; all of this I esteem very little if I but enjoy Christ."

Once Ignatius arrived in Rome, the authorities began to torture him, hoping that he might blaspheme Christ and sacrifice to the pagan gods. But all their torments only strengthened his faith in God. After a short while he was led to the inner arena to be cast before the lions. As he was being taken, he constantly spoke to the throng of onlookers of his precious Savior and their need to turn to Christ.

When the crowd was finally assembled, Ignatius was set alone in the middle of the amphitheater. With God-given boldness he raised his voice to the people and said,

> O Romans, all you who have come to witness with your own eyes this combat; know, that this punishment has not been laid upon me on account of any misdeed or crime; for such I have in no way committed, but that I may come to God, for whom I long, and whom to enjoy is my insatiable desire. For I am the grain of God. I am ground by the teeth of the beast, that I may be found a pure bread of Christ, who is to me the bread of life.

The mighty roars of two lions released from their pits immediately answered his words. They instantly set upon Ignatius, tearing and devouring his body. Within minutes the carnage was ended; hardly a bone was left.

Thus, early in the second century, godly Ignatius died, triumphant in faith, happy in the Lord, a martyr for Christ.

John Polycarp

Another martyr of the early church was John Polycarp. Committed to the purity of the gospel and deeply passionate about the things of God, Polycarp served as the bishop of the church at Smyrna for over fifty years. It wasn't until he was probably in his nineties that Polycarp faced serious persecution for his faith. In February of A.D. 156, the Roman authorities launched a serious attack on the church at Smyrna. Polycarp was willing to stay and face the persecution, but members of his church thought it best for him to go into hiding. So Polycarp withdrew from the city to a small farm. There in quietness and solitude he spent day and night in prayer for the believers in the city. As the days passed, the search for Polycarp intensified, and soon his location was made known. Arriving at the farm on the evening of February 22, armed soldiers apprehended Polycarp. He did not resist arrest, but simply replied, "May God's will be done."

After being taken into the amphitheater, Polycarp was encouraged to recant several different times. All he had to do was swear that Caesar was Lord. All he had to do was revile the name of Christ. But the reply from the lips of Polycarp came: "For eighty-six years I have been His servant, and He has done me no wrong. How can I blaspheme my King who saved me?"

At this the crowd went into a frenzy, shouting in unison that Polycarp should be burned alive. He was seized and bound to the stake. Soon wood and kindling were stacked around him and the fire was lit. As the flames licked up around him, the fire did not consume Polycarp's body.

So the crowd ordered the executioner to thrust him through with a sword. And so Polycarp died.

Polycarp did not pass from this life with fear or anxiety; rather, the eyewitness accounts record that he was inspired with courage and joy and that his face was filled with grace. In fact, just as the fires were being lit, Polycarp prayed aloud and gave thanks to God that he was privileged to meet a martyr's death for the glory of Christ:

> I bless you because you have considered me worthy of this day and hour, that I might receive a place among the number of the martyrs in the cup of your Christ, . . . May I be received among them in your presence today, as a rich and acceptable sacrifice. . . . For this reason, indeed for all things, I praise you, I bless you, I glorify you, through the eternal and heavenly High Priest, Jesus Christ.

Two Sisters

As the centuries passed, the Christian church grew in number and spread throughout the world. But accompanying this growth was continued persecution, especially in areas where false religions were deeply entrenched.

Nanilo and Aloida were two sisters who lived in Osca, Spain. Their mother was a nominal Christian who, after the death of her husband, repudiated Christ and married a devout Muslim. These sisters had the desire to live godly lives but were now unable to openly practice their faith due to the abuse of their stepfather. So when the opportunity arose, the girls went to live with their godly aunt. While under her care and instruction, the two sisters blossomed into strong young ladies with a deep passion for Christ.

"Without Christ there is no life, and without His knowledge there is nothing but eternal death."

It was not long, however, before their Christian testimony came to the attention of the Islamic city authorities. The sisters were arrested and brought before a judge. He attempted to draw them away from the Christian faith several times. He promised gifts, presents, and money. He promised the security of arranged marriages to prominent men in the town. Seeing that this was not affecting the girls, the judge then threatened them with tortures of the worst kind and, if they still would not recant, death by the sword.

In all this these two pious sisters were unmoved. Their response demonstrates their utter satisfaction in and loyalty to Christ:

> O judge, how is it that you command us to turn away from true godliness? God has made known to us that no one in the world is richer than Jesus Christ our Savior.

Nothing is more blessed than the Christian faith, by which the just live, and the saints have conquered kingdoms. For, without Christ there is no life, and without His knowledge there is nothing but eternal death. To dwell with Him, and to live in Him, is our only and true consolation. For the profit of the transient riches of this world, with which you thought you might allure us, we count as dung and loss, that we may gain Christ, because we know that everything under the sun, except Christ and true faith in Him, is vanity. And death, which you presented to us as the final terror, we will embrace because we know that thereby we go without delay to heaven, to Christ our Bridegroom, there to be embraced by Him inseparably, through His love.

Upon hearing their confession of Christ, the judge had the young sisters beaten and publicly humiliated. When it was obvious to all that the girls would still not deny Christ, the judge ordered their execution by sword. The fatal stroke was given, and on that day, October 22, A.D. 851, Nanilo and Aloida received their martyr's crowns, having triumphed in faith even unto death.

Hugh Latimer and Nicholas Ridley

During the mid-sixteenth century, God worked in Europe in a mighty way. The church, which for nearly 800 years had been floundering in the darkness of spiritual blindness and superstition, was visited with a reviving of the Spirit of God such that people were again being truly converted, and the Word of God was being freely studied and preached. This great moving of God is historically known as the Protestant Reformation. With a view to the supremacy of God in all things, the Reformation swept through much of the European continent within a single generation. And it wasn't long until the Reformation was felt in England, especially in the cities of Oxford and Cambridge. It was here, between the years of 1547-53, that the Reformation in England made great strides.

However, this growth of new life in the Protestant Church of England was hindered greatly by the rise to power of Queen Mary. The daughter of Henry VIII, Mary was devoutly Catholic and a hater of the Protestant Reformation. She persecuted the true church in England with such vehemence that many reformers fled to Germany and Geneva to find sanctuary. Many of those who remained in England were imprisoned or killed for their faith. It is estimated that Mary executed nearly 300 men, women, and children during her bloody reign.

Chief among those who gave their lives under Mary were two bishops: Hugh Latimer and Nicholas Ridley. These men grew up and ministered for years in the Catholic Church, but upon hearing the truths of the gospel were converted to Christ and embraced the Reformation. They were both diligent preachers and teachers of pure doctrine, devout in their private lives, and much beloved of their people. It is said that their flocks loved them the same way a child loves his father.

In September 1555 Latimer and Ridley were accused of heresy. That is, they were accused of not upholding the teachings of the Catholic Church. Their punishment was effected in three stages. Their first punishment was to be officially removed from the pastorate and stripped of their pastoral authority. The second was imprisonment. The third, if they had not yet recanted, was execution.

It was obvious from the start that neither Latimer nor Ridley had any thoughts of turning back from God. When asked to recant, Ridley replied, "You know my mind fully on this matter, and as for my doctrine, my conscience assures me that it was sound, and according to God's Word. And this doctrine I will maintain so long as my tongue shall move and breath is within my body, and to confirm this I am willing to seal the same with my blood."

"Be of good heart, brother, for God will either assuage the fury of the flame or else strengthen us to abide it."

The morning of October 15, 1555 came, and Latimer and Ridley were sentenced to be burned at the stake. Far from being despondent or afraid, these men were confident in the power of God to keep them even unto death. Their strong faith is seen in a comment Ridley made to a friend who was weeping over their impending death: "But quiet yourself, though my breakfast shall be somewhat sharp and painful, yet I am sure my supper will be more pleasant and sweet."

The two men were led to the north side of town to a large ditch over against Baliol College. As they walked, Ridley encouraged Latimer, "Be of good heart, brother, for God will either assuage the fury of the flame or else strengthen us to abide it." Upon reaching the place of execution both men knelt before the stake and offered a prayer of worship to the Lord. The authorities then offered the men one final chance to turn from their beliefs and embrace the Catholic Church. Ridley courageously replied, "So long as breath is in my body I will never deny my Lord Christ and His known truth; God's will be done in me!" Each man was then stripped of his clothing and left wearing only a simple shroud. They were then bound to the stake

Martyr Monument, Oxford, England.

with a chain, and a small bag of gunpowder was placed around each of their necks. As the wood was placed around them and they were being lit aflame, Latimer exclaimed, "Be of good comfort, Master Ridley, and play the man [act like a man]; we shall this day light such a candle by God's grace in England as, I trust, shall never be put out!" As the flames leapt higher both men were heard to cry out in loud, strong voices that God might receive their spirits.

In the words of one historian,

> Thus did these two pious divines and steadfast believers testify with their blood, the truth of the everlasting Gospel, upon which depends all the sinner's hopes of sal-

vation; to suffer for which was the joy, the glory of many eminent Christians who, having followed their Lord and Master through much tribulation in this vale of tears, will be glorified forever with Him, in the kingdom of His Father and our Father, of His God and our God.[4]

John and Betty Stam

The country of China has never been an "easy" place to take the gospel. Though there have been seasons during which missionary activity has flourished, it has come at a heavy price. This was certainly the case during the early part of the twentieth century.

After the Boxer Rebellion of 1900, China became very hostile to nearly all foreigners, especially missionaries. Missionaries were often attacked and beaten by Chinese officials. 50 percent of them abandoned China in 1927. Even the renowned China Inland Mission (CIM), started by the famous Hudson Taylor, was left with only a smattering of workers to man its more than seventy interior missions stations. It was during this time of crisis (1929) that the general director of CIM issued a call to all the sending nations, appealing for workers to come to China. They needed about two hundred new workers, and they needed them in less than two years.

Part of God's answer to the need in China was the sending of John Stam and Betty Scott. Both students at Moody Bible Institute, John and Betty met and developed a friendship while attending the school's prayer meetings for the CIM. It was not long before a deep love began to grow between them. However, they considered their call to the mission field more important than marriage. Thus Betty went to China in 1931 while John completed his schooling. Both wondered if their marriage was ever meant to be. Though seeing Betty leave was difficult, John's passion to proclaim Christ in China burned stronger. His address to his senior class captured this passion:

> Shall we beat a retreat, and turn back from our high calling in Christ Jesus; or dare we advance at God's command, in the face of the impossible? . . . Let us remind ourselves that the Great Commission was never qualified by clauses calling for advance only if funds were plentiful and no hardship or self-denial [were] involved. On the contrary, we are told to expect tribulation and even persecution, but with it victory in Christ.

John could not have known at that time the prophetic significance his own words.

John went to China in 1932, a year after Betty had set sail. In the good providence of God, Betty, who up until this time had been working in the Anhwei province, was sent back to Shanghai due to the political unrest of the region. While in Shanghai the two young missionaries met again, and it wasn't long before they were engaged, married, and serving with the CIM as a wonderfully happy couple. The birth of their first child in 1934 multiplied their happiness.

Later that fall, word came to the Stams that the mission station in Anhwei might be safe for work again. They were told that the Communist activity in the area had subsided and that the political and military threat was not nearly what it had been two years earlier. The local magistrate even gave his personal word of assurance to the Stams that Anhwei had been cleared of all Communist danger and that no one would do them harm. He could not have been more mistaken.

Arriving at their station in November, the Stams were, within a month, attacked in their home by Communist soldiers who demanded a $20,000 ransom from the CIM. The following is the letter John wrote to the CIM officials:

Dec. 6, 1934

Dear Brethren,

My wife, baby, and myself are today in the hands of the Communists, in the city of Tsingteh. Their demand is twenty thousand dollars for our release.

All our possessions and stores are in their hands, but we praise God for peace in our hearts and a meal tonight. God grant you wisdom in what you do, and us fortitude, courage and peace of heart. He is able—and a wonderful Friend in such a time.

Things happened so quickly this A.M. They were in the city just a few hours after the ever-persistent rumors really became alarming, so that we could not prepare to leave in time. We were just too late.

The Lord bless and guide you, and as for us, may God be glorified whether by life or by death.

In Him,

John C. Stam

The next day John and Betty were bound and marched to another town. It was a long, difficult trek. Adding to their physical pain were their fears for their daughter Helen. While the journey was in progress they often overhead their captors discussing whether or not to kill the child.

When they finally arrived, John and Betty were stripped of their outer garments and left for the night. The next day the Communists marched the missionaries, still bound, around the village, mocking them. After a crowd had gathered, John and Betty were taken to a grove of pine trees on top of a small hill. Suddenly, from the crowd of townspeople, ran a doctor who began beseeching the Communists not to kill the missionaries. He was taken off to be executed immediately. At this John Stam began asking the Communist authorities not to kill the poor doctor. Interrupting, the soldiers ordered John to kneel. John willingly kneeled to the ground, and with a flash of the executioner's sword his earthly life was ended. Betty, seeing the headless, bloodied body of her husband, slowly bowed her head and knelt to the ground. An instant later she joined her husband in the very presence of the Lord.

At the Stams's funeral, a Chinese evangelist spoke the following words:

> You have seen these wounded bodies, and you pity our friends for their suffering and death. But you should know that they are children of God. Their spirits are unharmed, and are at this moment in the presence of their Heavenly Father. They came to China and to Miao-shou, not for themselves but for you, to tell you about the great love of God, that you might believe in the Lord Jesus and be eternally saved. You have heard their message. Remember, it is true. Their death proves it so.[5]

Graham Staines and His Sons

Australian missionary Graham Staines was described as "a wonderful, gracious, self-effacing man of God, full of faith, confidence, and humility; warm-hearted, and a wonderful father."[6] He and his wife Gladys had three beautiful children: Esther, Philip, and Timothy. For over thirty years Graham Staines joyfully pursued a ministry to lepers in the Orissa district of India. They worked in the jungle amongst the Ho and Santhal tribes. Because of the stigma of the disease of leprosy, the lepers in this region were often unable to get proper medical attention. Graham daily showed the love of Christ to these needy people by treating and bandaging their wounds, instructing them in productive ways to earn a living, and sharing the message of hope and redemption through Jesus Christ. He started a leprosy home, taught in the village churches, translated the New Testament, and organized teams to evangelize the surrounding area.

Graham Staines was no stranger to regular persecution in Orissa, India. He knew of the attacks on Christians in villages just south of where he was located. He heard of the incident in a town nearby where the homes of 130 Christians had been set ablaze by those opposed to the Christian faith. He was familiar with the recent outbreak of church-burnings, attacks on missionaries, and stoning of Christian schools. And yet through all of this, Graham steadily pursued God's calling in his life.[7]

In January 1999, Graham traveled to an annual Christian camping retreat just outside the village of Manoharpur in Orissa. He was accompanied by his sons Philip (age 10) and Timothy (age 6). Graham was the camp speaker, and both father and sons were looking forward to a time of family fun and spiritual blessing. It was not meant to be.

Shortly after midnight on Saturday, January 23, an angry mob of nearly one hundred Hindu extremists carrying various weapons stormed the small village in search of Missionary Staines. Graham and his sons were sleeping in their jeep. Before they could wake up and realize what was happening, the fanatical mob had surrounded the jeep and began beating on it and shouting. The crowd then gathered straw and sticks and began stuffing them inside and underneath the jeep. Gasoline or kerosene was poured over everything. The vehicle was lit on fire. Eyewitnesses noted that as Graham attempted to open the door and windows to get out, the enraged killers would savagely beat him and his sons, forcing them back into the vehicle. There was nothing to be done. Within a few minutes the seething inferno had incinerated the jeep, and Graham and his two precious boys were dead. The charred bodies "were found locked in a final embrace in what must have been their last earthly prayer to the Author and Finisher of their faith—Jesus Christ."[8]

The remarks of his wife Gladys aptly summarize the legacy of this missionary martyr:

> I knew Graham was ready to lay down his life; he had a great love for the Lord.[9]

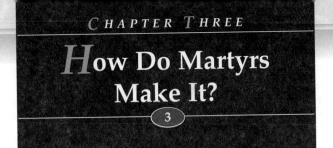

CHAPTER THREE

How Do Martyrs Make It?

3

Bunyan's Drama

John Bunyan, the great preacher and author of *The Pilgrim's Progress*, was born on November 30, 1628, in Elston, England. Bunyan was well acquainted with suffering for the cause of Christ. His pilgrimage with suffering began at the age of 32 when he was placed in prison because he refused to stop preaching the clear, undiluted gospel of Jesus Christ. Man's attempt to silence him separated him from his wife and from his four children, all of whom were under the age of ten, and one of whom was blind. This separation from his family was at times almost more than he could bear. While in the Bedford jail, Bunyan wrote the following words describing the heartache his imprisonment brought upon him:

> The parting with my wife and poor children hath often been to me in this place the pulling of the flesh from my bones; and that not only because I am somewhat too fond of these great mercies [referring to his wife and children], but also because I should have often brought to my mind the many hardships, miseries and wants that my poor family was like to meet with should I be taken from them, especially my poor blind child, who lay nearer my heart than all besides; O the thoughts of the hardship I thought my blind one might go under . . . would break my heart to pieces.

In the gracious providence of God, kind jailers would release Bunyan from time to time during his twelve-year prison stay for short visits with his family. But even though he was given these occasional "luxuries," the possibility of execution was a very real threat. Many people in that day had been put to death for doing no more than what John Bunyan had done.

While in prison Bunyan would often imagine himself dying a martyr's death. He did this to prepare himself for what might be the will of God for his future. This personal drama that he staged in his own mind's eye was to him vivid and emotionally charged. His worst fear was that he would ultimately in reality play his part as a martyr very badly. He feared that with weak and tottering knees he would collapse under the great weight of impending martyrdom. It was the great longing of his heart to possess that constant faith in and love for Christ that sustained the Christian martyrs he had come to respect so greatly.

Bunyan would with resolute determination picture himself wearing a blindfold while standing on the edge of the precipice of eternity. With the fragrance of heaven and the stench of hell in the air, he would stand ready to leap out, venturing all for God. Bunyan never experienced martyrdom, but he did venture all for God no matter the cost. What enabled Bunyan to think such bold thoughts for God? How can a person accept martyrdom graciously and courageously?

The Gospel's Power[*]

Romans 1:15-16 reveal what enables a man to make it to and through martyrdom with the same testimony of triumphant faith that Polycarp, Ignatius, Ridley, and Latimer had. In verse 15, Paul

---

[*] Much exegetical insight for this chapter was received from the following sources: (1) John Piper, *Not Ashamed of the Gospel* and *The Gospel Is the Power of God unto Salvation* (Minneapolis, MN: Bethlehem Baptist Church, 1998), audiocassettes. (2) Michael P.V. Barrett, *Romans #4* and *Romans #5* (Greenville, SC: Faith Free Presbyterian Church, 1993), audiocassettes. You may wish to consult these two sources for a more in-depth look at the argument of Romans 1:16.

informs the Roman believers that he is eager to come and preach the gospel to them. His eagerness was not diminished by his personal knowledge of how people often responded

How can a person accept martyrdom graciously and courageously?

to the gospel. To the Jews the gospel was a stumbling block, and to the Greeks it was foolishness (I Cor. 1:23); yet his eagerness remained intact. Man's response did not affect his readiness to preach the gospel to those who were in Rome.

How did Paul remain eager and ready to preach the gospel? Paul does not leave us to answer this question with our own guesswork. The first word of verse 16 informs us that Paul is answering the question for us: "For [because] I am not ashamed of the gospel of Christ." Paul traces his readiness to preach the gospel back to the fact that he is not ashamed of it. The gospel of Jesus Christ was everything to Paul. He was a man who had been separated graciously unto the gospel by Christ Himself (Rom. 1:1; Acts 9:1-6). His entire life and ministry revolved around the gospel.

The gospel, which is the good news of all that man can have in Christ Jesus, consumed Paul. His great passion was the good news that God justifies the sinner by faith in Christ and will ultimately glorify that same sinner together with Christ. One of Paul's most abhorrent thoughts was that he would ever pull back from this glorious gospel. In I Corinthians 9:16, Paul says with great sobriety, "For though I preach the gospel, I have nothing to glory of: for *necessity* is laid upon me; yea, *woe is unto me,* if I preach not the gospel!" Paul considered it personally disastrous for him to pull back from preaching the gospel.

One enemy of his boldness to preach the gospel was the temptation to be ashamed. Even though Paul was eager to preach, shame was a real temptation for him. Many of the Jews he faced

laughed at the "weakness" of his Messiah. They were expecting a strong, conquering messiah, not the meek and lowly Jesus of Nazareth. The Greeks thought the gospel was nonsense. They did not want to be bothered with such "absurd" ideas (see I Cor. 1:23). The possibility of being ashamed of the gospel was no trivial matter to Paul. He saw its dangers. In II Timothy 1:8, Paul commands Timothy, "Be not thou therefore ashamed of the testimony of our Lord, nor of me his prisoner: but be thou partaker of the afflictions of the gospel according to the power of God." Paul knew that being ashamed of the gospel would pull one back from a willingness to suffer hardship for the gospel. Just a few verses later in II Timothy, Paul informs Timothy that he himself is not ashamed (1:12).

What was it that kept Paul and will keep us from being ashamed of the gospel? What is it that will keep us from pulling back from a willingness to suffer persecution for the sake of the gospel? As if expecting that this is what his readers would want to know, Paul immediately identifies what it is that keeps him from being ashamed, "For [because] it [the gospel] is the power of God unto salvation" (Rom. 1:16*b*). Paul was kept from being ashamed of the gospel and pulling back from a willingness to suffer for it because he knew what it was—the *power* of God. Power is a wonderful thing to have on your side. It instills confidence and courage within you.

Notice that Paul does not refer to the gospel as being the power of God in general. He was not referring to the power of God to create the universe. Nor was he speaking of God's power to uphold all things that exist. The power of which he writes has a very narrow but significant field of application. It is a power that is exercised "unto salvation." It is a power that works directly for those who believe and has its end in their great and eternal benefit.

Now, in order to understand exactly how the gospel keeps us from being ashamed, there is one very important question that we

must take time to answer. When Paul says in Romans 1:16 that he is not ashamed of the gospel because it is the power of God unto salvation, does he mean that the gospel is the power of God to regenerate us, or that it is the power of God to bring about our glorification—the completion of our salvation? This is the crucial question for us to answer.

What was it that kept Paul and will keep us from being ashamed of the gospel?

The Power of God unto What?

It is best to answer this question with what historically has been called the analogy of Scripture. All this means is that we allow Scripture to interpret itself. When interpreting a somewhat ambiguous verse, we must go to those places in Scripture where the meaning is clear to see if they give us any insight for interpretation. This is the method we will use to answer our question.

Past or Future?

Scripture presents both past and future aspects of salvation. For instance, we find the past aspect of salvation referred to in Ephesians 2:8—"For by grace are ye saved through faith." In the Greek the text literally reads, "For by grace *you have been saved* through faith." By the verb tense we know that Paul is referring to the past aspect of salvation. "You have been saved, and you continue to be so" is the idea. However, the New Testament does have a strong emphasis upon salvation's future aspect—our entrance into complete salvation.

Consider Hebrews 9:28, where we are told not only that Christ came once "to bear the sins of many," but also that He is coming a "second time without sin unto salvation." The salvation spoken of here is obviously yet future since Christ has not yet returned. This verse clearly teaches that there is a very real future aspect of our salvation, which at this point in our spiritual pilgrimage we have not experienced.

But what about Paul? Does he ever emphasize this future aspect of completed salvation? In I Corinthians 1:18, he states that "the preaching of the cross is to them that perish foolishness; but unto us which are [being] saved it is the power of God." The verb (present passive) makes it very clear that believers are in the process of being saved. Our salvation is not yet complete. There is more of salvation to come for those who are believing. In II Thessalonians 2:13, Paul states that we were chosen by God "to salvation *through* sanctification of the Spirit." We learn from this verse that we are not yet experiencing all there is to experience of the salvation that is in Christ. We are still waiting for its completion. As the agent of sanctification, the Holy Spirit is ever bringing us closer to the completion of our salvation.

"But," someone may respond, "does Paul ever clearly refer to this future aspect of the completion of our salvation in the book of Romans?" Yes, he does. Note carefully the verb tenses of Romans 5:9-10:

> Much more then, being now justified by his blood, we shall be saved from wrath through him. For if, when we were enemies, we were reconciled to God by the death of his Son, much more, being [having been] reconciled, we shall be saved by his life.

Since as believers we have been justified, it is guaranteed that we shall be (future tense) saved from the future outpouring of God's wrath. There is a future day when the holy hurricane of

References to Glorification in Romans 8

- "quicken your mortal bodies" (8:11)
- "that we may be also glorified together" (8:17)
- "the glory which shall be revealed in us" (8:18)
- "the manifestation of the sons of God" (8:19)
- "the glorious liberty of the children of God" (8:21)
- "the adoption, to wit, the redemption of our body" (8:23)
- "them he also glorified" (8:30)

God's wrath will blow full force upon mankind; if we have been reconciled, we shall be saved from it.

The future completion of our salvation is a huge emphasis in Romans 8. Paul refers to our future glorification at least seven times in this chapter (8:11, 17-19, 21, 23, 30). In verse 19, inanimate creation itself is personified as eagerly waiting for the completed salvation of the sons of God. Verse 30 encourages us by affirming that the completion of our salvation is guaranteed.

We also find this future aspect of salvation in Romans 13:11, where Paul states that "now it is high time to awake out of sleep: for *now is our salvation nearer* than when we [first] believed." The salvation to which Paul refers is that final deliverance from this present evil world into the full realization of unending fellowship with God. What we learn from all of this is that the completion of our salvation is not merely *referred to* in Romans, but *emphasized*.

When we put all this data together, we find that we have warrant to say that the "salvation" of Romans 1:16 is referring not only to regeneration but also to the completion of our salvation. The gospel is not only the power of God to regenerate us, but it is also the power of God to bring us unto the enjoyment of completed salvation. But is this really what Romans 1:16 is teaching?

A Confirming Word

There is another key word that confirms our interpretation of Romans 1:16. Notice unto whom the gospel is the power of God unto completed salvation. It is unto "every one that believeth." Literally, it is "unto everyone *who is believing*." It will help us to see the significance of this literal rendering if we consider what it does not say. It does not say that the gospel is the power of God unto completed salvation to everyone who *has believed* (past tense). Rather, it says that it is the power of God unto salvation to everyone *who is believing* (present tense). The importance of the tense of the verb cannot be overlooked. It does not allow us to think of "believeth" as merely referring to a single, initial act of faith. Its emphasis is upon ongoing belief that can be described as the life of faith. In other words, the gospel is the power of God for those who are living by faith. The gospel brings only those who are daily believing it into the future enjoyment of eternal bliss. A completed salvation awaits only those who are daily resting in the gospel of God.

> *The gospel is not something of elementary value that we leave behind once we enter the high school of Christian maturity.*

First Peter 1:3-5 is the best parallel passage to Romans 1:16 in all of the New Testament. Verse 3 teaches that God has given us new life by the resurrection of Jesus Christ from the dead. Then it states that we who *have been given* new life *are being kept* by the power of God (the gospel) "through faith unto salvation [which is] ready to be revealed in the last time" (I Pet.1:5). Peter makes it

Links Between 1 Peter 1:3-5 and Romans 1:16

I Peter 1:3-5—Blessed be the God and Father of our Lord Jesus Christ, which according to his abundant mercy hath begotten us again unto a lively hope by the resurrection of Jesus Christ from the dead, to an inheritance incorruptible, and undefiled, and that fadeth not away, reserved in heaven for you, who are kept by the power of God through faith unto salvation ready to be revealed in the last time.

Romans 1:16—For I am not ashamed of the gospel of Christ: for it is the power of God unto salvation to every one that believeth; to the Jew first, and also to the Greek.

Think About It!

clear that when he refers to salvation he primarily has the completion of salvation in mind. If we link I Peter 1:5 with Romans 1:16, we have warrant to conclude that when Paul says that the gospel is "the power of God unto salvation," he means that the gospel is not only the power of God to regenerate us, but also the power of God to bring those who are ever believing in it unto completed salvation.

How Does the Gospel Do It?

The gospel is not something of elementary value that we leave behind once we enter the high school of Christian maturity. Believers always need the gospel. We cannot make it into the safety of eternity without it. We ever need the gospel because there are many obstacles in this life that stand between us and the completion of our salvation. All that is in the world—the lust of the flesh, the lust of the eyes, the pride of life—stands in our way, seeking to turn us from doing the will of the Father (I John 2:15-17). Only those who do "the will of God" abide forever (2:17). The world stands before every one of us as a massive obstacle (II Tim. 4:10).

Another obstacle that the gospel must conquer is unbelief. Hebrews 3:12 says, "Take heed, brethren, lest there be in any of you an evil heart of unbelief, in departing from the living God." Unbelief is such a dangerous threat to us that verse 13 goes on to say, "But exhort one another *daily,* while it is called To day; lest any of you be hardened through the deceitfulness of sin."

It is not enough for us merely to be converted by the gospel. There are too many deadly obstacles that stand between us and the completion of our salvation. These obstacles can be conquered only by the gospel's ongoing work in our lives. It and it alone is the power of God unto completed salvation. Therefore, in summary, if the gospel is indeed the power of God unto completed salvation, it is the gospel that gives us victory over every obstacle, including unbelief and the lusts of the world. Romans 1:16 makes it very clear that the gospel will not fail to bring every believer into the enjoyment of completed salvation.

"I Am Not Ashamed"

In Romans 1:16, the obstacle that Paul has been overcoming by the gospel is the temptation to be ashamed of the gospel. In this verse, Paul gives us a concrete example of the gospel's conquering power. If we can determine how the gospel gives believers victory over shame, we will then know how it gives victory over every obstacle to completed salvation, and also learn how believers like John Bunyan and Paul can face the prospect of a martyr's death graciously and courageously.

Keep in mind that the point Paul is making in Romans 1:16 is that the temptation to be ashamed *of the gospel* is overcome *by the gospel* because it is the power of God unto completed salvation. Therefore, Paul was unashamed of the gospel because of its relationship to the completion of his salvation. This is a very significant observation that will be seen more clearly if we consider a parallel experience in the life of our Lord.

Think About It!

Links Between Hebrews 12:2 and Romans 1:16

Hebrews 12:2—Looking unto Jesus the author and finisher of our faith; who for the joy that was set before him endured the cross, despising the shame, and is set down at the right hand of the throne of God.

Romans 1:16—For I am not ashamed of the gospel of Christ: for it is the power of God unto salvation to every one that believeth; to the Jew first, and also to the Greek.

"Despising the Shame"

Jesus came to earth to do the will of the Father (John 6:38). No one has ever faced as many obstacles to doing the Father's will as Jesus faced. He was tempted in every point as we are (Heb. 4:15). His life was fraught with the most intense temptation, grief, and anguish. Before Him stood the infinitely terrible curse of the cross and the shame it would hurl at Him. Christ marvelously became obedient to death, even the death of the cross (Phil. 2:8). No greater curse can be faced than that which Christ faced. No greater shame can be flung at a person than was flung at Christ. Yet He did not fail to do the will of His Father. Hebrews 12:2 says that Christ endured the cross and despised the shame. How was Christ able to do this? Can it be of any encouragement to us?

Hebrews 12:2 states very plainly that Christ endured the cross, despising the shame, for the sake of "the joy that was set before Him." Though the shame that was hurled upon Him looked very weighty from man's perspective, Christ looked upon it as very light in comparison to "the joy." Christ knew that the Father would show Him "the path of life" and that in His presence was "fulness of joy" and that at His right hand were "pleasures for evermore" (Ps. 16:11). This was the joy that was set before Christ. This was the joy that enabled Him to endure the cross and despise the shame.

The Joy of Final Salvation

The joy that the gospel wonderfully sets before us is the completion of our salvation in Christ who sits at the right hand of the Father. We can endure the temptation to be ashamed of the gospel when the joy of completed salvation is more than just words on a page. The gospel is the power of God unto the completion of our salvation partly because it gives us a clear view of the eternal joy awaiting those who are believing it. The joy that the gospel sets before us is a dominating joy. It conquers every shaming obstacle that confronts us.

If we become ashamed of the gospel, it is because we desire the joy that comes from man's acceptance more than we desire anything else (John 12:43). If the world's attempts to shame us are unsuccessful, it is because the joy of eternity with God looms very large on the horizon of this life. We, like Jesus, are able to despise the shame because the gospel sets before us the fullness of joy to be found in God's presence (Ps. 16:11).

Can you now better understand the meaning of Paul's words in Romans 1:15-16? "So, as much as in me is, I am ready to preach the gospel to you that are at Rome also. For I am not ashamed of the gospel of Christ: for it is the power of God unto salvation to every one that believeth."

The Martyr's Joy

How does a martyr or a prisoner like John Bunyan make it? By the design of God, the gospel is the window through which the saint gazes upon the pleasures of the next world, empowering him to face whatever lies ahead in the path of his Father's will. A martyr is a believer who despises the shame and endures suffering for the joy that is set before him.

Remember Stephen?

Do you remember what God revealed to Stephen in those last moments before he was stoned to death? Stephen, "being full of the Holy Ghost, looked up stedfastly into heaven, and saw the glory of God, and Jesus standing on the right hand of God" (Acts 7:55). Psalm 16:11 teaches that at God's right hand are "pleasures for evermore." Just before Stephen endured

The gospel alone can triumph over every evil that can possibly confront us in this life.

the immense pain of being stoned, God visibly set the joy of heaven before his eyes. Stephen was martyred with the awaiting joy of God's presence filling his heart. How else could Stephen pray in the last painful moments of his life, "Lord, lay not this sin to their charge" (Acts 7:60)? Stephen suffered martyrdom victoriously because of the joy that was set before him.

What About Us?

How can we possibly prepare for such a death if it is God's will for our lives? How can we like John Bunyan venture all for God no matter the cost? Again we go back to Romans 1:16, where it states that the gospel "is the power of God unto salvation *to every one that believeth.*" Please notice that completed salvation is only for those who are believing in the gospel day after day (*believeth* is present tense, which signifies continuous action). One of the primary points that Paul is making in Romans 1:16 is that the gospel is for believers. The gospel is what keeps believers believing unto the completion of their salvation. If we are trusting in the gospel of Jesus Christ, it *will* bring us all the way through temptation, the suffering of persecution, death, and ultimately the final judgment into the safety of eternal joy in the presence of God Himself.

So how can we be people who venture all for God no matter what obstacles lie ahead? By feeding upon the gospel day after day. Do you feed upon the gospel? Do you nourish your soul with the gospel of Jesus Christ? The gospel alone can triumph over every evil that can possibly confront us in this life. Are you daily standing in the gospel (I Cor. 15:1-2)? There is no victory in the Christian life apart from the gospel of Christ.

For a moment, forget the possibility that in God's plan you may become a martyr someday. If in your present circumstances you are to get victory over the temptations to sin that you face every day while at school or at home, it will be because you feed your faith day by day with the gospel of Jesus Christ. The means by which we feed our faith is by meditating upon the gospel as revealed in Scripture. In II Timothy 2:8, Paul tells Timothy to daily think of Jesus Christ, who has been raised from the dead. The word *remember* in II Timothy 2:8 refers to a continued keeping in mind. Paul is teaching us how to feed on the gospel— think on Christ. The gospel is what enabled Polycarp to die a martyr's death, and it is that same gospel that will enable you to gain victory over all the lusts of this present world (Titus 2:11-12). So whether you are to be a martyr or not, you cannot live without the gospel of Christ.

CHAPTER FOUR

Count It All Joy

4

> *Fear not, little flock; for it is your*
> *Father's good pleasure to give you*
> *the kingdom.—Luke 12:32*

The Dying Joy of Roy Orpin

The radio transmission recounted the details of the tragic death of missionary Roy Orpin[10]:

May 20, 1962—Thailand

Roy died last night at 10:15. Gillian [his wife] is there and has taken it very well. Christians in the town are helping a great deal. Hoping to have a funeral this afternoon at 4:00. . . .

On Wednesday, May 16, Roy had gotten together stores and supplies which they were going to use this rainy season. Left Pitsanulok on Lomsak bus and got off bus at kilometer 86. Arranged for some Meo carriers to meet him there. Started up the trail. Had not gone far when Roy stopped to change his clothes—clothes suitable for mountain climbing. The Meo carriers went on ahead. He was accosted by three men who had gotten on the bus and gotten off where he did. They were country Thai people [bandits]. They accosted Roy and held him up at gunpoint and demanded his

41

money. He gave it to them—500 baht. After robbing him they shot him twice—in the right side of his stomach and right side of his neck. Evidently the Meo heard the shots and came back. They did not touch Roy as they were very frightened but ran back to the road. In about a half hour they stopped a bus and the Lomsak driver went up and found Roy and got help of Meo to carry him down. Got back to Pitsanulok at 1:30 [P.M.]. Shooting probably happened around 11:00 A.M. Operated and sewed up stomach, diaphragm, colon and other things. Don Rulison and Arnold and Evelyn Melbourne arrived at hospital about 2:00 A.M. Thursday morning. Roy was very glad to see them. He was in much pain, but talked a bit. It looked very encouraging at times. At other times he would drop back into shock. Gillian arrived by rover from Manorom about 12:00 midnight Thursday the 17th. Yesterday morning, Saturday, Roy seemed better. Then doctor noticed his kidneys were not functioning properly. Kidneys stopped functioning at 6:00 P.M. Saturday evening and then it was just a matter of waiting until his heart stopped beating. He lived until 10:15 P.M. Saturday, May 19th.

A further glimpse into Roy's dying moments is recorded in a letter written by his wife Gillian shortly after his death. She recounts sitting by Roy's bedside and hearing him ask her to say the chorus "Jesus, I Am Resting, Resting." She leaned toward his ear and slowly recited,

> Jesus, I am resting, resting
> In the joy of what Thou art;
> I am finding out the greatness
> Of Thy loving heart.

Roy then smiled and whispered, "How good God is . . ." A short while later he passed into eternity, a martyr for Christ.[11]

*I*s This for Real?

When I first came across the story of Roy Orpin, two realities immediately stunned me. The first reality was that Roy suffered to the uttermost for the sake of Christ. The second, and more incredible reality, was that Roy counted it all *joy*.

Roy's Suffering

The first reality is certainly stunning, but one that we can get a handle on: Roy suffered. That's evident from much of what is recorded of his ministry.

The tribal language was hard to learn and speak; therefore his communication was often broken and misunderstood. The White Meo people were often rude and unresponsive. They gave him no privacy, arriving early in the morning for medical attention and often peering through his windows late into the night. The villagers who professed Christ often fell back into demonism and opium addiction. They needed constant spiritual watchcare. His house was once destroyed. His personal goods were often stolen or suddenly "borrowed" by the village people.

The geography of the area was formidable. Often it was cold. The trails were steep, muddy, and dangerous. The surrounding jungle was home to many predatory animals. All travel was by foot. Illness was a constant threat. Dogs roamed the streets. Pigs rooted under his house. There were problems with the water and drainage. The air stank. Fellowship with and encouragement from other missionaries

Does God really intend for His children to experience happiness while suffering?

was virtually nonexistent. The nearest missionary was a twelve-hour walk away. Visits were often needed but rarely enjoyed.

And if all this wasn't enough, consider the heartbreak of his final days. Roy had been married just over thirteen months. His wife, Gillian, had been sent to the hospital because she was due to deliver their first child. Roy was then shot by Thai bandits and left to bleed to death on a jungle trail. Finally, he made it to the hospital, only to die a few days later. All this, and he was just twenty-six years old!

Let's make no mistake about it, Roy Orpin gave his life for the service of Christ amid pain and difficulty. Roy's suffering was real.

Roy's Joy

The second reality of this story is even more stunning than the first and much more difficult to figure out: Roy suffered *joyfully*.

When we read over the difficulties of Roy's ministry to the White Meo people and the account of his death, we are moved by Roy's love and dedication; our hearts are touched with the sorrow and the pain of it all. But there's

something that ought to absolutely shock us. Think back to Roy's deathbed request. Notice the words he wanted fixed in his mind and the mind of his wife: "Jesus, I am resting, resting in the *joy* of what Thou art . . . How good God is . . ."

This is so shocking to us because it is the exact *opposite* of what most of us would be thinking at that moment. He's been through incredible hardship, is on the brink of death, and the legacy he wants to leave with his still-pregnant wife is the assurance that he is counting it all joy and trusting in the goodness of God! How can this be? How can Roy Orpin be experiencing joy in the midst of horrible tragedy? How does a man who has lost so much to the adversities of life rest in the joy of Christ and the goodness of God at the point of death?

The reality of joy in suffering, communicated so poignantly in the ministry and death of Roy Orpin, is a difficult reality for us to get a handle on. It seems so foreign; so strange; so impossible.

Is This Reality in the Bible?

It's one thing to acknowledge the reality of suffering. But the idea of joy *in* suffering is certainly more difficult to believe. The question we must ask is this, "Does God really intend for His children to experience happiness while suffering?" Or, to put it another way, "Do we find 'joy in the midst of suffering' presented in the New Testament?" The answer: everywhere. A brief overview of some passages that link joy and suffering should be enough to show us that this concept permeates the New Testament. Consider the following:

> *Blessed* are they which are persecuted for righteousness' sake: for theirs is the kingdom of heaven. *Blessed* are ye, when men shall revile you, and persecute you, and shall say all manner of evil against you falsely, for my sake. *Rejoice*, and be exceeding *glad*.—Matthew 5:10-12

> And they departed from the presence of the council, *rejoicing* that they were counted worthy to suffer shame for his name.—Acts 5:41

And not only so, but we *glory* in tribulations.—Romans 5:3

Most *gladly* therefore will I rather *glory* in my infirmities, that the power of Christ may rest upon me. Therefore I take *pleasure* in infirmities, in reproaches, in necessities, in persecutions, in distresses for Christ's sake.—II Corinthians 12:9-10

Yea, and if I be offered upon the sacrifice and service of your faith, I *joy*, and *rejoice* with you all.—Philippians 2:17

Who now *rejoice* in my sufferings for you.—Colossians 1:24

And ye . . . received the word in much affliction, with *joy* of the Holy Ghost.—I Thessalonians 1:6

For ye had compassion of me in my bonds, and took *joyfully* the spoiling [stealing] of your goods.—Hebrews 10:34

Looking unto Jesus the author and finisher of our faith; who for the *joy* that was set before him endured the cross, despising the shame.—Hebrews 12:2

My brethren, count it all *joy* when ye fall into divers temptations.—James 1:2

But *rejoice*, inasmuch as ye are partakers of Christ's sufferings; that, when his glory shall be revealed, ye may be glad also with exceeding *joy*.—I Peter 4:13[12]

Where Does This Joy Come From?

So we've seen that the suffering is real. And we've seen that the New Testament confirms that joy *can* exist in the midst of agony. The Scriptures even seem to indicate that joy in suffering is normal for the believer. But wouldn't you admit that happiness in the midst of pain does *not* seem normal or natural? It doesn't seem like there's any possibility that joy and suffering would ever go together.

How do we embrace pain for Christ's sake as our pleasure?

So how do we deal with this seeming paradox that the New Testament presents? How do we get a handle on this teaching of the Scripture, this "joy in suffering"? In other words, where does this joy come from? What motivates it? What is it rooted in? How do we embrace pain for Christ's sake as our pleasure?

A Great Reward

A key passage that will help us with this is Matthew 5:10-12. Note how it begins:

> Blessed are they which are persecuted for righteousness' sake.

What Does This Mean?

The word "blessed" communicates the idea of *happy* or *fortunate* or *approved*. This is an absolutely shocking statement that rivets our attention. We think to ourselves, "Why in the world should someone who is persecuted for righteousness' sake be happy? It sure doesn't sound like a happy time to me!" How can this be? And this is our great paradox, isn't it?

Well, the verse goes on to state the reason:

> For [because] theirs is the kingdom of heaven.

The reason they should have joy in the midst of their suffering is that they are promised something incredible: they will inherit the kingdom!

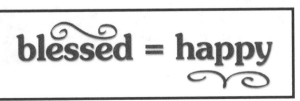

blessed = happy

Christ goes on in this passage to extend this blessedness to those who seek to follow Him. Verses 11-12 read,

> Blessed are ye, when men shall revile you, and persecute you, and shall say all manner of evil against you falsely, for my sake. Rejoice, and be exceeding glad.

Note our word *blessed* again. Christ is saying that you are to be happy [considered fortunate] when men cast insults at you, harm you, and spread misinformation about you behind your back. As a matter of fact, He says you're supposed to be filled with joy and gladness over this!

And again, it's at this point that our minds tend to freeze up. This just doesn't sound right, does it? It just doesn't seem normal. It seems too incredible to believe that Christians are to be considered fortunate when they are killed; happy when they are beat up; and approved of God when they are ridiculed, shamed, and maligned.

Yet Christ gives the reason for this. Again the sufferer is encouraged in verse twelve to fix his eyes on the greatness of a future reward:

> For [because] great is your reward in heaven.

The implications of this are remarkable. Think about it: Christ is telling us that the coming reward for those who suffer well for the sake of His name is so tremendously wonderful that the persecution now can be endured with joy. One way we can rejoice in suffering is to gaze on the greatness of our future reward. The incredible magnitude of the coming reward makes the present persecution seem small in comparison.

A Key Motivation: Greater Suffering, Greater Reward[13]

What is even more motivating about verse 12 is that it seems to hint that there is some kind of quantitative correlation between the amount of suffering endured now and the depth of reward enjoyed in the future. In other words, the greater the suffering now, the greater the reward then.

> *One way we can rejoice in suffering is to gaze on the greatness of our future reward.*

Think about it like this: How would Christ's words motivate us to suffer joyfully if the glories of heaven were experienced to the same degree by those who suffered for their faith as well as those who did not? It seems like the suffering would be kind of useless, doesn't it? It seems like the best thing to do would be to just "grit it out." It certainly doesn't motivate us to embrace suffering with joy. *But* if we knew that all our sufferings were working for us a greater and greater reward in heaven, the words of Christ would carry a hundred times more force in motivating us to embrace suffering joyfully.

Prove It

The wondrous idea that there are different degrees of happiness in heaven can be supported by other Scriptures (Matt. 19:29; Luke 19:17-19; Rom. 2:6-7; I Cor. 15:41; II Cor. 9:6).[14] There is one text, however, that directly supports what we've just discussed in Matthew 5:12. Note the meaning of Paul's statement in II Corinthians 4:17-18:

> For our light affliction, which is but for a moment, worketh for us a far more exceeding and eternal weight of glory; while we look not at the things which are seen, but at the things which are not seen: for the things which are seen are temporal; but the things which are not seen are eternal.

The word we want to focus in on is the word "worketh" from verse 17. This word could properly be translated by any of the following: *achieves, brings about, prepares, effects.* Now take any of those words and plug it into verse 17. Do you see what Paul is saying here? Paul is indicating that our present afflictions are the means to a greater experience of future glory! And this is exactly what Christ is intimating back in Matthew 5:12: the future reward grows as present suffering is endured. If this is so, then we really have a tremendous reason to "rejoice, and be exceeding glad"; when we suffer persecution for Christ's sake, our heavenly reward is increasing!

> And every one that hath forsaken houses, or brethren, or sisters, or father, or mother, or wife, or children, or lands, for my name's sake, *shall receive an hundredfold,* and shall inherit everlasting life.—Matthew 19:29

A Loose End—Another Reason to Rejoice

Now this is all well and good, but we still need to discuss the last part of Matthew 5:12:

> Rejoice, and be exceeding glad . . . for so persecuted they the prophets which were before you.

So how does this fit in? How does the fact of the persecution of the prophets in days gone by motivate me to have joy in my persecution now? How does remembering *their* sufferings help me rejoice in *my* sufferings? There are at least three ways.

I Belong to Christ

Thinking about the persecution of the prophets confirms my place among God's people. This confirmation comes from answering two questions: "What did the prophets suffer for?" and "What am I suffering for?" The answer is the same: for the sake of righteousness. One needs only to look at Hebrews 11:36-39 to see that the Old Testament martyrs died for the cause of righteousness (see also I Kings 18:13, 19:10; Neh. 9:26; Jer. 26:23). So if I am suffering for righteousness' sake, I am in the same standing as those great heroes of the past. Their God is my God.

"Blessed are they which *have been* persecuted. . ."

Did believers suffer for their faith in the Old Testament? Hebrews 11:36-38 makes it clear that many did:

> . . . and others were tortured, not accepting deliverance; that they might obtain a better resurrection: And others had trial of cruel mockings and scourgings, yea, moreover of bonds and imprisonment: They were stoned, they were sawn asunder, were tempted, were slain with the sword: they wandered about in sheepskins and goatskins; being destitute, afflicted, tormented; (Of whom the world was not worthy:) they wandered in deserts, and in mountains, and in dens and caves of the earth.

This means I'm real. I'm genuine. I am one of His. This gives me joy.

I Am Not Alone

Another reason (closely linked to the above) that remembering the prophets causes joy in suffering is that it reminds me that I am not alone in my suffering. A great cloud of witnesses has gone before me in suffering. I am not unique, or abnormal, or forsaken. Others (no doubt more godly than I) have suffered too. Looking to the prophets' suffering confirms that I belong to the same family as those radical, risk-taking messengers of God from days gone by. I am not alone. I am not abandoned. This, too, gives me joy.

Remember Their Reward

The key reason Christ encourages us to look to the prophets as a means of birthing joy in our hearts is found in the context of Matthew 5:10-12 itself. The prophets "who were before you" are obviously those from the past; that is, their suffering is not currently taking place; it occurred centuries ago. Therefore the prophets (and other past martyrs) meet perfectly the description given back in verse 10–"Blessed are they which are persecuted for righteousness' sake." In Greek, the construction of Matthew 5:10 is somewhat different than in English. We would properly translate it like this: "Blessed are the ones who *have been persecuted* for righteousness' sake." The prophets have already been persecuted. According to the end of verse 10, those who have been persecuted inherit "the kingdom of heaven." Thus, the prophets who suffered in the past inherited the kingdom of heaven. Thus, we could paraphrase the meaning of verse 12 like this:

Rejoice and be filled with gladness! Why? Because your reward in heaven is great. How so? Well, do you remember the godly martyrs of the past? They were persecuted just like you . . . and they inherited the kingdom!

So when Christ points us back to the prophets, He actually points us toward the future. To remember what they went through is to remember what they gained in the end. A look backward to the past is actually a look forward to the future. To focus our minds on their sufferings is to focus our faith on the coming reward.

Wrapping It Up

So in Matthew 5:10-12, Jesus gives the reason for rejoicing in suffering, namely that the reward in heaven is great. These words of Christ are echoed elsewhere in the New Testament. Paul said in Romans 8:18, "For I reckon that the sufferings of this present time are not worthy to be compared with the glory which shall be revealed in us." He states in Philippians 3:8, "Yea doubtless, and I count all things but loss for the excellency of the knowledge of Christ Jesus my Lord: for whom I have suffered the loss of all things, and do count them but dung, that I may win Christ."

Paul's point? There is no comparison between the affliction now and the glory to come. His faith was armed with the knowledge that suffering is "working" a reward whose greatness grows with every hardship endured. The apostle Peter confirms this same perspective when he writes, "But rejoice, inasmuch as [to the degree that] ye are partakers of Christ's sufferings." Why? Peter goes on, "That, when his glory shall be revealed, ye may be glad also with exceeding joy" (I Pet. 4:13).

Therefore, you can experience joy in suffering as you fix the eyes of your faith on the glorious inheritance of your future reward. "It is a faithful saying: For if we be dead with him, we shall also live with him: If we suffer, we shall also reign with him" (II Tim. 2:11-12).

Final Thoughts to Fuel Our Joy

You can see from what we've learned in this chapter that joyfully enduring persecution really comes down to what we focus our faith on. Back in Chapter 3 we asked, "How does a martyr make it?" The answer: "By faith in the gospel." If we are trusting in the gospel, it will bring us all the way through persecution and martyrdom. This chapter says the same thing, just in a different way. "How does a martyr make it *joyfully?*" The answer: "By faith in the future reward." And that future reward is an integral part of "final salvation" mentioned in Chapter 3.

These thoughts are beautifully expressed in I Peter 1:3-6,

> Blessed be the God and Father of our Lord Jesus Christ, which according to his abundant mercy hath begotten us again unto a lively [living] hope by the resurrection of Jesus Christ from the dead, to an inheritance incorruptible, and undefiled, and that fadeth not away, reserved in heaven for you, who are kept by the power of God through faith unto salvation ready to be revealed in the last time. Wherein [In this] ye greatly rejoice, though now for a season, if need be, ye are in heaviness through manifold temptations.

Notice at the end of these verses Peter states that the believer rejoices even though he is suffering. Why should he rejoice? Well, look back at the beginning of the verses. Peter states three glorious reasons why the believer should rejoice:

- God has begotten us [saved us] and given us a living hope.

- God has provided us an inheritance [reward] that will not decay, is uncontaminated by sin, and is permanently beautiful.

- God has promised to keep the believer to the day of final salvation.

We are to rejoice in our sufferings because there is a wonderful future in store for us on that day when we are finally brought into the safety and rest of final salvation! From Peter's perspective, faith in the gospel and faith in the coming reward are really one and the same. To focus on one is to live in the reality of the other.

What are you focused on day after day? Is it the worries of life? The pressures of school? The frustrations of spiritual failure? Have you faced persecution because you try to live a passionate life for Christ? Are you discouraged because you've been teased or picked on? Do you do without many nice things because your family is in the ministry? Are you ridiculed when you share the gospel with a lost person? Are you tempted to give up because it seems the more you live for God, the more you endure hardship?

If so, then remember this: suffering joyfully comes down to fighting for faith. Rather than focusing on the pain and agony of persecution or hardship, learn to believe the promises of God. Fuel your faith by daily feasting on the gospel. Live by a faith that is fixed on a future reward. You will find that this kind of living will result in a faith-filled joy that triumphs in your day of adversity.

But without faith it is impossible to please him: for he that cometh to God must believe that he is, and that he is a rewarder of them that diligently seek him.—Hebrews 11:6

CHAPTER FIVE

Death: Not to Be Feared

5

The Death Sentence

Imagine seeing a graphic execution such as David Hackston, a faithful Scottish believer of the 17th century, experienced for his undying faith in Christ. Part of David's suffering was knowing that his execution would be drawn out and extremely painful. When the nightmarish day arrived, he was led away to suffer as an animal to be butchered. He courageously endured the cutting off of his right hand, but when the hangman had problems severing his left hand at the forearm, David earnestly requested that it be severed at the joint, and so it was. He was then pulled to the top of the gallows where he was strangled but let down before life left him. The hangman then took his knife, and after cutting out David's intestines, cut into his chest, removed his heart, and waved it around on the end of his knife for all to see.[15]

> *"God be praised! Death no longer appears as the king of terrors, but seems to invite me to partake of some unknown joys."*
> —Lord Henry Otto of Bohemia, upon his execution

If you knew that it was God's will for you to die just as David Hackston died, how would that make you feel? You would most likely feel a level of fear bordering on terror. There are at least two fears that stories of execution like this can create within us. First, there is the fear of death itself. Needless to say, no one who reads this chapter knows what it is like to experience death. It is natural for us to fear the unknown, especially when it is something like death. We do not usually view death as a friendly visitor, but as a dark phantom intruder. Who in his right mind really wants to face death? The very thought of its approach can inspire fear.

Second, there is the fear of *dying,* which is different from the fear of death. Have you ever heard someone say that he is not afraid of death but of dying? What did he mean? He probably meant that he knows from the Scriptures that as a believer to be absent from the body is to be present with the Lord (II Cor. 5:8). But the process of dying can be excruciatingly painful. So although we may have conquered the fear of death itself, it is an entirely different thing to conquer the fear of dying.

If you are not careful, such fears can keep you from living the radical, God-centered lives that the Scriptures call you to live. This kind of living puts you on a path that may end in painful suffering and death. The people of this world cannot begin to understand the choice to live this kind of life. To them, death is a terrifying reality about which they would rather not give any serious thought (Heb. 2:15). Why choose the path of suffering and a potentially premature death when you can get your fill of eating, drinking, and being merry in this life (Luke 12:19)? The fear of death is a great enemy of God-centered living. Therefore, you must come to grips with these death-related fears and attack them with the Scriptures. We must fight fear with the Scriptures because radical God-centered living comes from a Scripture-dictated viewpoint of life and death.

Preparing to Fight

In II Timothy 4:7, Paul states near the end of his life that he had fought the good fight of faith. How was Paul able to fight well? How did faith triumph over the fear of death in Paul's life? With what did Paul feed his faith so that it would not crumble under the fear of death? The answer is found in Philippians 1:20-

21. What did we say in Chapter 3 about how a martyr makes it to and through death? He makes it with the gospel. We learned from Romans 1:15-16 that the gospel is not only the power of God to regenerate us but also the power of God to conquer every obstacle we face en route to the full experience of our salvation in Christ. Death is a real obstacle that seeks "to separate us from the love of God, which is in Christ Jesus our Lord" (Rom. 8:39). The Scriptures also teach that the last enemy of the saints to be destroyed is death (I Cor. 15:26).

We have taken time to review what we have learned from Romans 1:16 because there is an important connection that we must not fail to identify between it and Philippians 1:20-21. Both texts give us strategies for being unashamed as believers. If we understand the connection between the two texts, we will find the Christ-centered viewpoint of life and death we desperately need. So let's ask some questions that will help us identify the connection between these two verses.

According to my earnest expectation and my hope, **that in nothing I shall be ashamed,** but that with all boldness, as always, so now also Christ shall be magnified in my body, whether it be by life, or by death. For to me to live is Christ, and to die is gain. -Philippians 1:20-21

For I am not ashamed of the gospel of Christ; for it is the power of God unto salvation to every one that believeth; to the Jew first, and also to the Greek. -Romans 1:16

Before Reading On

Write out what you think being unashamed means and then check yourself with what follows.

What Does It Mean to Be Unashamed?

One way Paul demonstrated that he was not ashamed of the gospel was his readiness to preach it. So it appears that according to Romans 1:15-16 being unashamed of the gospel means being eager to preach it. Is this all there is to it? Is desiring to preach all there is to being unashamed?

This question bears serious consideration because texts such as Philippians 1:15-16 refer to those who preach Christ out of envy, strife, and contention; or II Corinthians 4:1-2 where Paul contrasts his ministry with those who handle the Word of God deceitfully. We learn from these two texts that it is possible to preach the gospel and not be rightly related to it. To be unashamed of the gospel we must be rightly related to it. Therefore, we do not go far enough when we say that being unashamed of the gospel means heaving a ready eagerness to preach it, since one can preach it and not be in right relationship to it.

Going Further

Philippians 1:20-21 reveals what being unashamed means. Notice what Paul does *not* say in verse 20—"According to my earnest expectation and my hope, that in nothing I shall be ashamed, but that with all boldness, as always, [I will preach the gospel]." Paul's confident expectation (hope) is not that he will preach. *Paul's hope was that Christ would be magnified in his body* "whether it be by life, or by death" (1:20).

So, being unashamed of the gospel does not just affect your public, verbal witness. Being unashamed is an eagerness for Christ to be magnified in the life as a whole, preaching being just one compartment of that life. The kind of preaching that Paul refers to in Romans 1:15 comes from a life that desires Christ to be magnified no matter what the cost.

Therefore, when Paul exhorts Timothy (II Tim. 1:8) not to be ashamed of the testimony of Christ, he is mainly exhorting him to magnify Christ in his body whether it be by life or by death. Let's see if this is clear in the text. Notice that Paul commands Timothy not to be ashamed but to be a "partaker of the afflictions of the gospel according to the power of God." According to this verse, not being ashamed of the testimony of our Lord means being willing to share in (being a partaker of) the same sufferings other believers are experiencing on account of the gospel. Not being ashamed means I am willing to embrace the path of suffering even if it ends in my death. Is not this what Paul means when he says his hope is that Christ be magnified in his body even in death (Phil. 1:20)?

Paul was a man who wholeheartedly embraced the path of suffering and was calling Timothy to do the same. Being unashamed of the gospel is more than just being eager to preach it. Not being ashamed of the gospel means that I embrace the afflictions of the gospel. How can someone possibly embrace this hard road when the fear of death and dying stand before him like fierce, towering giants?

Paul's Strategies for Fighting Shame, or Fear

Both Romans 1:16 and Philippians 1:20-21 teach us how to fight being ashamed of the gospel, which is really a fight against fear. If Paul had not been ready to preach the gospel to those at Rome (Rom. 1:15), it would have been because he feared the shame. But instead, he, like Jesus, despised it (Heb. 12:2). These two texts teach us how Paul fought fear in general as well as how he fought the specific fear of death.

At this point we need to determine whether or not Paul is giving us in these two texts two strategies for fighting fear. In Romans 1:16, Paul states that he is not ashamed of the gospel because "it is the power of God unto salvation." In Philippians 1:20-21, Paul states that he is not ashamed because to him "to live is

Christ, and to die is gain." So, do we have one or two strategies for fighting fear?

The fear destroyer in Romans 1:16 is a sure understanding of what the gospel is—"the power of God unto salvation." In Philippians 1:20-21, the fear destroyer is a Christ-centered understanding of life and death—"to live is Christ, and to die is gain." Are these really two different ways to destroy fear?

In answering this question we must first realize that you cannot affirm Romans 1:16 concerning the gospel and not affirm Philippians 1:20-21 concerning Christ. How can this be true? In Romans 1:1, Paul refers to the gospel of Romans 1:16 as "the gospel of God," that is, the good news that comes from God Himself. Then in verse 9 he refers to it as "the gospel of his [God's] Son." In other words, God's gospel is His good news to

Text	Fear Destroyer
Romans 1:16	An understanding of the gospel
Philippians 1:20-21	An understanding of life and death.

man about His Son. Later, in Romans 15:15-16, Paul states that he was given grace that he might bring God's good news to the Gentiles. Then again in Romans 15:19, Paul says that he has "fully preached the gospel of Christ."

The point we must not miss is that *the gospel in its entirety points to the Person of Christ.* Christ is the beginning and the end of the gospel. Christ is God's good news to sinners. The gospel is a telescope that has one object in its sight: the glory of Christ. In II Corinthians 4:3-4, Paul says that the gospel is hid from the lost by the god of this world (Satan) lest the light of the gospel of the glory of Christ should shine unto them.

You cannot separate what Paul says in Romans 1:16 from what he says in Philippians 1:20-21 because to know and embrace the gospel is to know and embrace Christ Himself. If you feed and meditate upon the gospel, you feed and meditate upon Christ. So, if the gospel is for you a fear destroyer (Rom. 1:16), you will say that to you to live is Christ and to die is gain (Phil. 1:21). Romans 1:16 and Philippians 1:20-21 essentially give us a single strategy for fighting fear.

Fighting to Win

We learn in Philippians 1:20 that instead of being ashamed, Paul earnestly expected that Christ would be magnified in his body, whether by life or by death. It is very clear in this verse that Paul enjoyed victory over the temptation to be ashamed and over the fear of death. The prospect of enduring shame and suffering unto death did not deter him from earnestly living a life that magnified Christ. Obviously, Paul loved something more than he loved the comforts of this life, more than he loved life itself. How could Paul give himself to a way of life that to many looks suicidal? What enabled Paul to let go of earthly comforts and joyfully embrace the possibility of dying as a martyr? How could the threats of death and dying hold no power over him?

To Live and To Die[16]

One of the most important words in Scripture is the word *for*. It is often used throughout Scripture to identify a cause or reason for a statement that comes before. The *for* of Philippians 1:21 is used in this way. It introduces the reason that Paul could say verse 20 with such confidence. "Christ shall be magnified in my body, whether it be by life, or by death. *For* [because] to me to live is Christ, and to die is gain." Paul was confident that Christ would be magnified in his continued living and eventual death because of what living and dying was to him.

Word Connections

Notice the word connections between verses 20 and 21. The word "life" in verse 20 corresponds to the word "live" in verse 21. Also, "death" in verse 20 corresponds to "die" in verse 21. These word connections tell us that whatever Paul is saying in verse 20, he is continuing in verse 21. The *for* of verse 21 introduces a reason or cause for verse 20. Now make sure that you see the significance of the word *for*, combined with these key word connections. We learn that Paul expected (hoped, 1:20) that Christ would be shown to be great (magnified) while he lived (1:20) because of what life was to him (1:21), and when he died (1:20) because of what death was to him (1:21). We learn in these two verses that Paul was freed from the bondage of the fear of death because of his Christ-centered viewpoint of life and death.

> Philippians 1:20 According to my earnest expectation and my hope, that in nothing I shall be ashamed, but that with all boldness, as always, so now also Christ shall be magnified in my body, whether it be by **life** or by **death**
>
> 1:21 For [because] to me to **live** is Christ and to **die** is gain.

Detective Work

Now comes our most difficult task as interpreters. We must determine what the phrases "to live is Christ" and "to die is gain" mean. They are Paul's reasons for confidence that Christ *will* be magnified in his body whether by life or by death. We were able to determine this without looking outside these two verses. But we cannot determine what these two phrases mean without looking outside of these two verses. So what are we to do?

Let me illustrate. What if you went to an estate auction where all the belongings of a widower who recently died and had no surviving relatives were being sold to the highest bidder, and you happened to get your hands on one of this man's many diaries. As you read through it you find a statement he makes that fascinates you. He wrote, "For to me to live is basketball." Since you have always been a fan of basketball, you are very curious as to what he meant.

Did he mean that for him to live is to play basketball? Or did he mean that for him to live was to coach basketball? Or was he just a huge fan of the game? "For to me to live is basketball" could mean many different things, and it is the only reference to basketball in that section of the diary that you could find. So what should you do next if you really want to find out what it means? Well, you decide to purchase that diary and as many of the others as you can afford. Then you begin reading through each diary, looking for any reference to basketball that you can find and recording all the data.

As you do this you learn that he was one of the best high school coaches in the state. He won eight state championships and had dozens of players who ended up playing for Division I schools. He was annually invited to speak at nationally known coaching clinics and wrote a book about coaching basketball that continues to be rated as one of the best. After hours of research in his diaries you would then be able to give a lecture on this man's life and explain with great confidence and authority what this man meant when he said, "For to me to live is basketball."

Researching Paul

This is what we must do with "to live is Christ" and "to die is gain" if we really want to grasp what Paul actually means. We will begin by working our way backwards through Philippians 1:21. What does Paul mean by "to die is gain"?

The most important thing we can do is see if Paul uses the word *gain* or any form of it elsewhere in his writings in a similar context referring to Christ. As we read through the book of Philippians, we find Paul telling us about the things he greatly valued before his conversion. He took great pride in the fact that he was "circumcised the eighth day, of the stock of [a member of the people of] Israel, of the tribe of Benjamin, an Hebrew of the Hebrews [meaning he had retained the Hebrew language and customs], as touching the law, a Pharisee; concerning zeal, persecuting the church; touching the righteousness which is in the law, blameless" (3:5-6). These are the things that Paul valued the most in life before he was converted.

Yet in verse 7, Paul says, "But what things *were gain* to me, those I counted loss for Christ." So, the things in verses 5 and 6 that Paul once considered to be gain he now considered to be loss. In other words, Paul no longer valued those things. This is no small declaration. Let the weight of what Paul is saying hit you full force. The things that he once valued *more than anything else in this world* he no longer valued at all!

Something like this does not just happen. People just do not wake up one morning and trash all their treasures. You find a person's

Treasures hold the heart prisoner.

treasures, and you know exactly where his heart is (Luke 12:34). Treasures hold the heart prisoner. Hearts love treasures and will not give them up without a world war of sorts. Only something that is deeply profound in its worth can cause a man to completely trash his value system. What was it that caused Paul to throw out his valued treasures?

The answer—Paul found a superior treasure, something that was so valuable that he considered all else to be as refuse (Phil. 3:8). Paul was like the man who, when he found a treasure buried in a field that he had daily passed without having any interest in it, hid the treasure and for joy sold all he owned in order to buy the field and possess the treasure (Matt. 13:44). Paul came to consider the so-called treasures of Philippians 3:5-6 as trash because he found an infinitely superior treasure. What was this superior treasure?

Notice carefully what verse 7 says, "But what things were gain to me, those I counted loss *for Christ.*"

Christ was the superior treasure that freed his heart from the trash heap that was masquerading as a to-die-for treasure. Paul's heart now valued Christ and where He is— sitting at the right hand of God (Col.

3:1) where there is fullness of joy and pleasures forevermore (Ps. 16:11).

So, when Paul says "to die is gain," is the gain that he is referring to actually Christ? Let's go back to Philippians 1:21 and continue to read on in the context to see if our insights from Philippians 3:5-7 fit. Paul says, "For to me to live is Christ, and to die is gain. But if I live in the flesh, this is the fruit of my labour: yet what I shall choose I wot not. For I am in a strait betwixt two, having a desire to depart, and to be with Christ; which is far better" (Phil. 1:21-23). When Paul says that he has a desire to depart (1:23), what does he mean? He means that he has a desire to depart this life—die—and be with Christ. Why does he want to depart and be with Christ? Because in Paul's mind, to do so "is far better" (1:23). In other words, being with Christ is better than anything he could ever experience or enjoy in this life!

> *There is nothing in the universe that even begins to compare to His value.*

Now, if we plug all this data into Philippians 1:21, this is what Paul is essentially saying—as far as he is concerned, to live is Christ and to die is *Christ* (gain). Why substitute *Christ* for the word *gain?* Because Christ was Paul's gain! For Paul, dying was gain because it transported him into the very presence of the One he treasured more than anything else. What we should learn from Paul is that there is nothing more valuable than Christ. He is the superior treasure in comparison to all other treasures. There is nothing in the universe that even begins to compare to His value.

Why Did We Walk Backwards?

Why have we worked our way backwards through Philippians 1:21? Let's answer this question by remembering that to say "to die is gain" is to say "to die is Christ." There is no difference in meaning because Christ is gain. Now, does this help us in our understanding of what "to live is Christ" means? Yes, it opens for us a window through which we can see what really made Paul tick. Christ was everything to Paul. So much so that he could say that "to live is Christ." But what does "to live is Christ" actually mean?

We have already observed in Philippians 3:7 that what things were at one time gain to Paul, he now considered to be loss for Christ. He is not saying that he merely considered those things loss at some point in the past and since then his values have once again changed. The exact meaning of verse 7 is that he considered and continues to consider those things loss for Christ. This meaning is clearly articulated in verse 8: "Yea, doubtless, and I count [I am considering] all things but loss for the excellency of the knowledge of Christ Jesus my Lord." Christ was Paul's constant treasure. He was ever counting all things loss in comparison to the surpassing value of knowing Christ. Paul states that he did this in order that he may win Christ (3:8). The word *win* is the same Greek word translated *gain* in Philippians 1:21. Paul's entire life from his conversion onward was all about gaining Christ.

Therefore, "to live is Christ" means to enjoy fellowship with Christ, to find satisfaction in knowing Christ, and to pursue your eternal joy in Christ. In other words, to say, "To live is Christ" is to say that Christ is your constant, all-satisfying treasure. We foolishly rob ourselves of joy and satisfaction if we cannot say for ourselves, "To live is Christ."

Two Questions to Answer

All of the interpretive fruit that we have labored to produce must now be put to good use. If our present study is to reach its conclusion, we must use our interpretive

When we give up our lives in order to gain Christ, we prove His exceeding value.

data to answer two questions. First, how is Christ magnified in the martyrdom of a saint? Second, how does Philippians 1:20-21 help us conquer death-related fears?

Paul's confident expectation was that Christ would be magnified even in his death (Phil. 1:20). The word *magnify* means to show to be great. It is not the showing to be great that a microscope does when it takes something that is really small and makes it look big. *Magnify* is better illustrated with what a telescope does. A telescope sets its sight on something far away that looks like it is very small and shows it as it really is—incredibly massive. Paul was confident that in his death he would show Christ as He is—awesomely great!

So how is Christ shown to be great in a martyr's death? The answer comes when you put Philippians 1:20 and 21 together. "Christ shall be magnified in my body, whether it be by life, or by death. For to me to live is Christ, and to die is gain." If we take the *life* and *live* components out of these two verses, the answer is even clearer. "Christ shall be magnified in my body . . . by death. For to me . . . to die is gain."

What we learn is that Christ is shown to be great in our dying when to us dying is gain. When we give up our lives in order to gain Christ, we prove His exceeding value. When you can say, "Let goods and kindred go, this mortal life also," you show that you have no greater treasure than Christ!

When the unbelieving world sees a man or woman give up all earthly goods, comfort, and life for Christ, it cannot help but conclude that Christ must be exceedingly great. How can someone joyfully give up the American Dream to die a martyr's death like Jim Elliott did? Jim Elliott did this because he knew that in heaven he had "a better and more enduring substance"

In Summary

- "To live is Christ" means that you are experiencing Christ as gain while you are living.
- "To die is gain" means that in death you gain Christ.

(Heb. 10:34). He wrote, "He is no fool who gives what he cannot keep [the American Dream] to gain what he cannot lose [Christ]."

The death of a martyr is a spiritual telescope. It sets its sight on the all-glorious Son of God and brings His unsurpassed greatness up close for all to see. Martyrdom is to the spiritual world what the Hubble Space Telescope is to the physical universe. The Hubble Telescope amazes us with images of galaxies and stars that testify to the unfathomable size of the universe. In like manner, the martyr's death testifies to "the excellency of the knowledge of Christ Jesus" (Phil 3:8). So, Christ is shown to be great in our dying when to us dying is gain.

In Nothing Terrified

Our second question is: How does Philippians 1:20-21 help us to conquer death-related fears? The ability to endure great pain has much to do with perspective—with how you perceive the big picture of reality. For example, why in the world would a woman choose to experience the incredible pain of giving birth to a child? Some women endure the pain of childbirth over and over again. Susanna Wesley, the mother of John and Charles Wesley, had eighteen children. How does a woman conquer the fear of great pain and bring a child into this world? The answer in part is perspective. She considers all that is involved in bringing a child into the world and concludes that the sufferings of childbirth are not worthy to be compared with the joy that is set before her in the child.

Perspective is powerful. In Romans 8:18, we find that Paul was convinced "that the sufferings of this present time are not

One More Look

Philippians 1:20-21—According to my earnest expectation and my hope, that in nothing I shall be ashamed, but that with all boldness, as always, so now also Christ shall be magnified in my body, whether it be by life, or by death. For to me to live is Christ, and to die is gain.

worthy to be compared with the glory which shall be revealed in us." This verse teaches that Paul took his mental balance and put the prospect of future glory in one pan and then the sufferings of this world in the other and found that the sufferings of this world *did not even begin* to tip the balance. In Paul's mind and in reality, the weight of glory far outweighed the weight of suffering.

In II Corinthians 4:17, Paul refers to "the sufferings of this present time" as "our light affliction." How can Paul refer to what David Hackston experienced as being a "light affliction"? Paul answers by saying that our "light affliction worketh for us a far more exceeding and eternal weight of glory" (4:17). David Hackston's suffering worked to give him more glory than he could possibly imagine. This is reality. This is why Paul can refer to the sufferings of this present time as light.

This is the perspective that every Christian must have regardless of how his or her life ends. Why be afraid to risk all for the kingdom of God when you know by the Word of God that suffering works for you an "eternal weight of glory"? This is how Christ wants us to live and think. In Luke 12:32, Jesus says, "Fear not, little flock; for it is your Father's good pleasure to give you the kingdom." According to Jesus, the reason we should not be afraid to live a God-centered life is that the Father is well-pleased to give us the kingdom, which is where we will enjoy glory (I Thess. 2:12). It is His joy to give it to us!

Can you see this perspective radiating through Philippians 1:20-21? Paul was literally ready to give his life in service to Christ because *to him* to die was gain. The "to me" of Philippians 1:21 tells us that this was Paul's personal perspective. This perspective was not merely what he had heard others talk about or what he had read in a book on martyrdom. It was his perspective! To Paul, dying was gain! Notice that he placed no qualifications on the phrase "to die." It mattered not to Paul how he died—whether it was a quick death at a chopping block, or a torturous death spanning hours of time, or a death by natural causes—because death to him was the gateway to eternal gain in Christ.

Notice this same fear-conquering perspective surfaces later in verses 28 and 29. Paul tells the Philippians that they are to be "in nothing terrified" by their adversaries (1:28). Paul is telling the Philippians that nothing their adversaries say or do is to terrify them. This is a pretty weighty expectation that Paul is placing upon them. What perspective can Paul offer them that might conquer terror?

Verse 29 answers this question for us. "In nothing terrified by your adversaries [1:28] . . . For [because] unto you it is given in behalf of Christ, not only to believe on him, but also to suffer for his sake" (1:29). The word *given* refers to a gracious gift. Paul identifies two gracious gifts that are given to us by the Father. First, God graciously gave us faith in Christ. We would all agree that to believe on Christ is a wonderful gift. Second, God graciously gave us suffering for Christ's sake. Should we view this gift as any less precious than the first?

How can Paul say that suffering for Christ is a precious gift? Romans 8:17 teaches that if we suffer with Christ, we will also be glorified together with Him. Second Timothy 2:12 states that if we suffer with Christ, we will also reign with Him. Suffering is a great gift because it is not mainly about pain. Any pain we may experience is but for a moment. Suffering is a gift because it is mainly about gain!

According to Philippians 1:28-29, the knowledge that suffering is a gracious gift from God conquers fear. Suffering works for believers. Do not permit the fear of death and dying to keep you from God-centered, Christ-magnifying living. Meditate upon the Scriptures. Feed upon the gospel, which in the Scriptures reveals the salvation to be obtained "in Christ Jesus with eternal glory" (II Tim. 2:10). Read, study, and meditate upon "the word of the truth of the gospel" which will give you hope and in turn motivate you to give yourself to the kingdom of God through deeds of love (Col. 1:4-5).

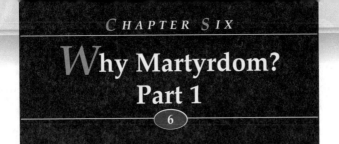

CHAPTER SIX

Why Martyrdom?
Part 1

6

The Execution

The prisoner was ordered to kneel.

So this is how it's going to end, John thought as he slowly lowered himself to the ground. His knees sank into the sodden straw and mud. It felt cool on his skin, almost refreshing.

"Unshackle him," barked the executioner at the guards. With a jolt and a clank, the chains fell off John's wrists and ankles.

John looked at the pile of rusty links beside him. Each one seemed to bring back a memory of the past several months in prison. The darkness, the filth, the stench, the sleepless nights, the hunger, the pain, the loneliness . . .

Imprisoned for preaching Jesus the Christ, he thought. *Imprisoned for calling sin, sin.* John almost laughed to think of it. He couldn't remember a time in his life that he hadn't been preaching. It just seemed like the message burned within his bones. And to think of the places his preaching took him! First the cities, then the villages, and finally way out in the middle of nowhere. And yet the people still came.

"Put your head down, and don't budge an inch. I've got to make this a clean one." The executioner smiled sarcastically. His oily face glistened in the torchlight.

John bent his head low to the ground. A moist, earthy smell filled his nostrils. It reminded him of the river back home.

How many people had he baptized there that summer? It seemed the line of converts was always smaller than it should have been. Poor farmers, mostly. And some beggars. A few prostitutes from town. And that priest from the upcountry. Mostly, people just watched. Some, of course, came to debate. *What did they expect to see anyway?* And what a strange sight it must have been! The offscouring of society turning to the Lord because of a wild-eyed country preacher. *I was just doing what the Lord would have me do,* John chuckled to himself.

"Are you going to lie there laughing? Say something!" snarled the executioner.

Last words? John's mind snapped back to reality. The glint of the executioner's sword caught his eye. It was long and smooth; well greased; honed to a razor's edge.

His mind went back to those special words of Jesus, those words that Jesus had spoken just for him. Those words that had been a comfort time and time again as he sat in this dark, lonely hole in the ground. "Blessed is he who does not take offense at Me."

What a wonderful confirmation, John thought. *What a tremendous vindication.* All the hardship he had suffered, all the destitution, all the abuse, all the pain . . . It was worth it all!

And to have it end this way . . . ?

"Well," grunted the executioner, staring down, "we don't have all night."

Raising himself slightly, John spoke in almost a whisper: "You know, I was never worthy to unlatch His sandals anyway. May He ever increase, as I decrease. . . ."

Perplexed, the executioner glanced at the other guards. They shrugged their shoulders and looked back sheepishly. John simply lowered his cheek to the dirt; a distant, faraway look in his eyes; a broad, happy smile on his face.

Is Martyrdom Meaningless?

Does martydom make sense?

A Wasted Death?

Let's consider John the Baptist. How did he die? You'll remember that it wasn't very glamorous. As a matter of fact, it is one of the most pathetic scenes in all of the New Testament.

John was imprisoned by King Herod because he preached against sin. You see, Herod had married his brother's wife, Herodias. It was a sick, sinful situation. And all the people knew about it. John the Baptist took a stand for righteousness and preached against the king's adultery. When this was made known to the royal couple, Herodias, the queen, was incensed. No camel-hair-clad country preacher was going to insult her like that and get away with it! She told Herod, her husband, to have John killed. The only problem was that Herod feared John; he knew that John was a just man, and frankly, he kind of liked John's style. But to appease his wife, he had John thrown in prison.

A few months later, Herod threw himself an extravagant birthday party. He invited nobles and military officers, and basically anybody who was somebody. It was a grand affair, and all eyes were on Herod, that is, until the daughter of Herodias came in. It wasn't long until all the guests were transfixed by her mystical, sensual dance. Her charms worked especially well on the host himself. Herod (no

> ### Want to Know More?
>
> The story of John the Baptist's death can be found in the Gospels. Check out Matthew 14:3-12 and Mark 6:14-29.

doubt intoxicated) was so taken by her that he granted her a wish—up to half his kingdom; and this was his great mistake. For you see, Herodias had already coached the girl what to ask for. It was time for "sweet revenge."

The request came back to Herod: she would like the head of John the Baptist delivered immediately on a platter. Herod was sorry in his heart, but since he had made an oath to the girl, and in order to save face with his guests, he sent word to the prison. A short time later John the Baptist was dead.

Is This Fair?

When we hear an account like that, we are tempted to think that John was dealt a horribly unfair lot in life.

Think about it. John had spent a life in faithful service to the Lord. He had denied himself nearly every pleasantry that life had to offer so that he could fulfill his commission as the forerunner of the Messiah. He dressed in rough clothing. He ate the basest of foods. He never sought his own glory or prestige. He humbly stepped aside when the Lamb of God arrived on the Judean scene.

And what is the reward for all that faithfulness to God? Being thrown in jail because the queen didn't like his preaching! Then several months rotting away in a prison cell. And finally, decapitated because some spineless aristocrat made a ridiculous promise to a dancing girl!

"What is wrong here?" we ask. "This doesn't make sense! How could a loving God allow this? Why in the world would He let His faithful servant be treated in such a shameful way? What possible purpose could there be in letting a lone man endure such an awful fate? This can't be fair!"

The Certainty of Suffering*

If we are to learn anything from the death of John the Baptist, we must come to grips with the sobering reality it presents: Christians suffer, and, in some cases, Christians suffer excessively. It may take different forms at different times for different people, but the truth still remains that believers get persecuted. They get killed. They get beaten bloody. They get

---

*The authors are indebted to the following sources for portions of the organization and exegetical insight of the remainder of this chapter and Chapter 7: (1) Joni Eareckson Tada, and Steve Estes, *When God Weeps* (Grand Rapids: Zondervan, 1997). (2) John Piper, *Let the Nations Be Glad* (Grand Rapids: Baker Books, 1993).

mocked. They get locked away in filthy prisons. They get raped. They get robbed. They get falsely accused. Christians from all ages have faced suffering and martyrdom. History testifies to it. Volumes have been written to document it. Whole organizations exist for the sole purpose of tracking the persecution of the Church throughout the world.

Christians suffer, and, in some cases, Christians suffer excessively.

So What Does the Bible Say About It?

But all of that is really irrelevant if the Word of God doesn't come to bear on the issue. Does the Scripture address the persecution of believers? Or, let's make it more personal—"Does God's Word teach that I will suffer and possibly even die a horrible death like John the Baptist?"

The Seed of Martyrdom

The seed of martyrdom is planted at the moment of conversion. The expectation of suffering for the believer is presented in the very call of God to the sinner. Christ states, in no uncertain terms, that "whosoever will come after me, *let him deny himself, and take up his cross,* and follow me. For whosoever will save his life shall lose it; but whosoever shall lose his life for my sake and the gospel's, the same shall save it" (Mark 8:34-35). Christ goes even further in Luke 14:26: "If any man come to me, and hate not his father, and mother, and wife, and children, and

Paul's Story

The seed of martyrdom was planted at the moment Paul was converted. Indeed for Paul, suffering was part and parcel of being a Christian.

Suffering Promised

"But go thy way: for he is a chosen vessel unto me, to bear my name before the Gentiles, and kings, and the children of Israel: For I will show him how great things he must suffer for my name's sake."
—Acts 9:15-16

Suffering Fulfilled

"Of the Jews five times received I forty stripes save one. Thrice was I beaten with rods, once was I stoned, thrice I suffered shipwreck, a night and a day I have been in the deep; In journeyings often, in perils of waters, in perils of robbers, in perils by mine own countrymen, in perils by the heathen, in perils in the city, in perils in the wilderness, in perils in the sea, in perils among false brethren: In weariness and painfulness, in watchings often, in hunger and thirst, in fastings often, in cold and nakedness."
—II Cor. 11:24-27

brethren, and sisters, yea, *and his own life also,* he cannot be my disciple."

Christ is certainly calling for a forsaking of self in these verses. No one who is unwilling to die to his selfish desires can follow Christ. We must have an attitude that despises anything that would compete with Christ.

However, let us not miss the clear implication of adopting that attitude. Those who follow Christ do not value their lives in the same way that they used to. They have a radically different perspective on what it means to live in this world. They no longer spend their days trying to protect their life. Their view is this: "I'll do whatever it takes to follow after Christ, even if it means taking up a cross"—even if it means dying. No man can be a disciple of Christ who is unwilling to come to terms with the suffering it might entail.

The Example of Christ

If there was ever a person who suffered unjustly at the hands of godless men, we all must agree that it was the Lord Jesus. Furthermore, no one who has ever lived has suffered as painful and shameful a death as Christ. Yet His suffering was no mistake. It was a divine necessity.

> And he began to teach them, that the Son of man must suffer many things, and be rejected . . . and be killed.
> —Mark 8:31

> For even the Son of man came not to be ministered unto, but to minister, and to give his life a ransom for many.
> —Mark 10:45

> But first must he suffer many things, and be rejected of this generation.—Luke 17:25

> And he said unto them, with desire I have desired to eat this passover with you before I suffer.—Luke 22:15

> Searching what, or what manner of time the Spirit of Christ which was in them did signify, when it testified beforehand the sufferings of Christ.—I Peter 1:11

Now, if it was needful that our Lord suffer so, why should we think it unusual (or unfair!) that we should suffer, who call ourselves after His name? It was the Lord Himself who told the disciples that "the servant is not greater than his lord. If they have persecuted me, they will also persecute you" (John 15:20). The Scripture would have us know that "it is enough for the disciple that he be as his master" (Matt. 10:25). That Christians will suffer persecution is certain because it is the very example of our Lord whom we are to follow and emulate. If they did it to Him, it should be no surprise when they do it to us. As a matter of fact, we should expect it to happen "because Christ also suffered for us, *leaving us an example,* that ye should follow his steps" (I Pet. 2:21).

It is not *likely* that you will suffer as a Christian; it is *assured*. The persecution and suffering that true believers face is not optional because it is not an accident. Suffering is certain because it is our God-directed destiny. Consider the following:

> For I will show him [Paul] how great things he *must* suffer for my name's sake.—Acts 9:16

> Confirming the souls of the disciples, and exhorting them to continue in the faith, and that we *must* through much tribulation enter into the kingdom of God.—Acts 14:22

> And if children, then heirs; heirs of God, and joint-heirs with Christ; *if so be* that we suffer with him, that we may be also glorified together.—Romans 8:17

> For as the sufferings of Christ abound in us, so our consolation also aboundeth by Christ.—II Corinthians 1:5

> For unto you it *is given* [graciously granted] in the behalf of Christ, not only to believe on him, but also to suffer for his sake.—Philippians 1:29

> That no man should be moved by these afflictions: for yourselves know that we are *appointed* [destined] thereunto.—I Thessalonians 3:3

> Wherefore let them that suffer according to the *will of God* commit the keeping of their souls to him in well doing, as unto a faithful Creator.—I Peter 4:19

Suffering is God's will for His children. It's a certainty we cannot deny.

But Why?

We've spent the last several pages showing that the Bible assures the Christian that suffering and persecution will happen. But this still doesn't deal with the heart of the questions we asked at the beginning of the chapter, does it? In fact, you might be thinking that it makes the situation worse. If suffering is to be expected

Does God Ever Discipline?

Would a loving God ever chasten His children with suffering?

Find the answer in Hebrews 12:4-11.

Think About It!

by *all* who believe, then suffering now seems all the more pointless.

Someone might say, "You know, I can understand how God might let a disobedient Christian suffer. He's getting the punishment that he deserves. You 'reap what you sow,' right? God is just chastening him. I can even understand why Christ had to suffer. His suffering was unique. It was for the purpose of redeeming sinners. But we're not talking about wayward Christians or the Lord Jesus. We're talking about faithful preachers and missionaries and innocent followers of Christ who really love the Lord. Why is it that suffering is certain for them? Aren't things supposed to go better when God is on your side? Wouldn't a loving Father keep bad things from happening to his children? Why does all this misery have to occur?"

> *But the question is not "Why do Christians get persecuted or martyred for the sake of Christ?" The real question is "Why do Christians suffer at all?"*

These are good, but difficult questions. As a matter of fact they are some of the most perplexing questions a believer is capable of asking. But the question is not "Why do Christians get persecuted or martyred for the sake of Christ?" The real question is "Why do Christians suffer *at all?*" The question is not just "Why did missionary so-and-so have his house burned down by fanatics?" No, the real questions go much deeper. They go to the core of the believer's state in a lost world. "Why did Grandma get cancer?" "Why did Laura die in a car wreck?" "Why did I get a headache that made me fail my test?" "Why do these bad things keep happening to me?"

The "Who" of Suffering

Before we can ever begin to understand the "why" of suffering, we must face up to the "Who" of suffering. To make sense out of all this seeming mess, we must get a handle on who or what is behind it all. We have only three options.

Option #1—The Occurrence of Fate

A church on the coast is completely razed by a hurricane. A Christian mother of four is put in the hospital for weeks due to some food poisoning she picked up at a restaurant. The church van is hit by a drunk driver, killing three teens and critically injuring two others. Are these bad things the result of fate?

By "fate" we mean the idea that these bad things happen "on accident" or "by chance." This would include things like the catastrophes of nature, car wrecks, and bad things that happen as the result of human error (like falling off a cliff) or moral wickedness (like a terrorist blowing up a plane). Fate is just about anything in the world around us that is out of our control.

So is fate to blame? Bad weather and bad people? On the surface it might seem like it. We've all heard situations like the scenarios above. It seems like there was nothing anyone could have done to prevent it. It was just a stroke of bad luck.

But let's test this in the light of one of the worst cases of "bad things" happening to a "good man." Let's look at Job. As you read this account (Job 1:1–2:13), you will note that bad weather and wicked men play a large part in Job's downfall. Look at all the "chance" happenings: the Sabeans destroyed the oxen and donkeys (and farm hands), lightning struck the sheep (and shepherds), the Chaldeans killed the camels (and servants), and a tornado blew down the house, killing all ten of Job's children. What are the odds of all this happening on *the same day?* Then there was the unexplained sickness of boils and sores that covered Job from head to toe. Job was reduced to sitting on an ash heap, scraping the open wounds with a piece of a broken pot!

Is this just a case of really bad luck? It seems like it. Does the Bible say that Job's problems were a result of bad weather and wicked men? Yes, on the surface, it does. But we must go further.

Option #2—The Attack of Satan

The second option we have in analyzing "who" is behind the suffering of believers is to look at the most wicked being in all the universe—Satan. Certainly his track record of doing bad things to God's people is pretty clear. Didn't he trick

Eve into eating the forbidden fruit (Gen. 3:1-8)? Isn't he called the father of lies (John 8:44)? Isn't he the "accuser" of the brethren (Rev. 12:10)? Isn't he the "adversary" who goes about like a roaring lion seeking to devour Christians (I Pet. 5:8)? Then surely all the bad things that happen to Christians must come from him!

Well, let's test this by our case study in the book of Job. Did Satan cause Job's sufferings? It appears so. Job 1:12 says that "all" Job had was put in Satan's power. In chapter 2, verses 5 and 6, Satan was even given power to bring sickness on Job's body. Now, we are not directly told in this passage how much control Satan has over nature, but from all appearance the Sabeans, the lightning, the Chaldeans, the tornado, and the boils were all manufactured by Satan, who *really* had it in for Job. Consider II Corinthians 4:4 (Satan is the "god of this world," blinding people to the gospel); II Timothy 2:26 (Satan sets snares for people and makes them do his will); and I John 5:19 (the whole world lies under the power of Satan), and you may rightfully conclude that Satan is the one who caused Job's sufferings. But we must go further yet.

Option #3—The Will of God

At the most basic and fundamental level, all suffering and evil that happens to a believer comes by the loving decree of God.

How can this be? Well, let's go back to our benchmark story. We have seen that Fate

Job, who of all people should be screaming for answers regarding suffering, goes directly to the source of his problems and credits them to the will of God.

played its role, right? And Satan played his role by using Fate, right? But wait a minute. Who gave Satan the authority to do what he did? Wasn't it God (see Job 1:12; 2:6)? We must note this well: Satan did not act against Job of his own volition. He had to first get clearance from the One who controls all things—God.

Think About It!

Who Is Responsible for The Death of Christ?

Check out Acts 2:23-24 for an answer that might surprise you.

Whether it was to attack Job's livelihood or to attack Job's body, Satan first had to get God's permission.

We are quick in our spirit to defend against the thought that God had anything to do with Job's sufferings. Yet look what Job *himself* said regarding the horrible disasters that came upon him:

> The Lord gave, and the Lord hath taken away; blessed be the name of the Lord. In all this Job sinned not, nor charged God foolishly.—Job 1:21-22

> Shall we receive good at the hand of God, and shall we not receive evil [adversity]? In all this did not Job sin with his lips.—Job 2:10

Job, who of all people should be screaming for answers regarding suffering, goes directly to the source of his problems and credits them to the will of God. And lest we still think to ourselves, "No, Job! It wasn't God! It was Satan. He had this deal going, and he stirred up the weather and those wicked men to come against you," the Scripture says two times that Job "did not sin with his mouth" in attributing to God's decree the work of Satan and the happenings of fate. And if there's *still* any doubt, Job 42:11 states,

> Then came there unto him all his brethren, and all his sisters, and all they that had been of his acquaintance before, and did eat bread with him in his house: and they bemoaned [consoled] him, and comforted him over all the evil [adversity] that the Lord had brought upon him. . . .

Other Scriptures also show that God is in control of all that happens; both what appears to be good and what appears to be bad:

> And the Lord said unto him [Moses], Who hath made man's mouth? or who maketh the dumb, or deaf, or the seeing, or the blind? have not I the Lord?—Exodus 4:11

Out of the mouth of the most High preceedeth not evil [woe] and good [well-being]?—Lamentations 3:38

Shall there be evil [adversity] in a city, and the Lord hath not done it?—Amos 3:6

We must conclude that at the deepest level, the ultimate "who" behind our sufferings is God Himself. There is no other option.

CHAPTER SEVEN

Why Martyrdom? Part 2

7

What Is God Really Like?

For many people it is very unsettling to think of God as purposefully allowing bad things to happen to His children. The pain they see is so graphic; so intense; so heartbreaking; so personal. "If this is what the suffering is like, what must the One behind it all be like?" they reason. "He is either very evil to allow it, or too weak to prevent it."

Both assumptions are dead wrong.

The Scripture teaches a threefold mystery:

> * God is a Being of infinite goodness.
>
> * God is a Being of infinite power.
>
> * God is a Being who ordains suffering for His eternal purposes.

Stop and reread those three statements. It is absolutely vital that we affirm each of these teachings of Scripture. They are absolutely crucial to a proper view of suffering. If we don't get this straight, we will never come to grips with our suffering, and we will end up despising and hating God.

God—Infinite Goodness

The Scripture is replete with descriptions of the goodness of our God. Theologians use the term *goodness* to encapsulate the plethora of vocabulary the Bible uses to communicate this aspect of the character of God. God's goodness includes attributes like His:

Holiness: God is completely separate from all sin; He is completely morally upright; He transcends all created things.

Righteousness: God always abides by the perfect standard of His Law; He never directs someone to do wrong.

Justice: God is fair in all that He does; He is not partial; He doesn't play favorites.

Genuineness: God is real; He is true.

Veracity: God's description of reality is accurate. He is not out to fool people.

Faithfulness: He never fails; He always keeps His word; He never breaks a promise.

Benevolence: God has a tender concern for His children.

Grace: God shows favor to people to meet their needs, even though they are unworthy. God does favors for people and never requires repayment.

Mercy: God has pity on those in misery.

Longsuffering: God is not quick to judge sin but patiently invites people to repent.[17]

When we look at these stunning characteristics of God, we have to conclude that He is the most tenderhearted, loving Being in all the universe, especially when we consider how each of those attributes has been manifested to us personally. Furthermore, when you consider how this God has suffered on our behalf, it is nearly overwhelming. That a perfectly content, eternal God should bend to our need in providing salvation in Christ—the King perishing for the sake of His kingdom—is truly incomprehensible. Our God is a God of infinite goodness. We see it in our salvation. We see it every time we take a breath.

He is the most tenderhearted, loving Being in all the universe.

The Lord is good to all: and his tender mercies are over all his works.—Psalm 145:9

God—Infinite Power

Not only is He a God of infinite goodness, but He is a God of infinite power. We say He is *omnipotent* (all-powerful). God can do whatever He wants, whenever He wants, however He wants.

But our God is in the heavens: he hath done whatsoever he hath pleased.—Psalm 115:3

God . . . made the world and all things therein, . . . he is Lord of heaven and earth.—Acts 17:24

Who hath measured the waters in the hollow of his hand, and meted out heaven with the span, and comprehended the dust of the earth in a measure, and weighed the mountains in scales, and the hills in a balance? . . . It is he that sitteth upon the circle of the earth.—Isaiah 40:12, 22

With men this is impossible; but with God all things are possible.—Matthew 19:26

We see the omnipotence of God in nearly every chapter of the Scriptures. He creates worlds. He orchestrates history. He delivers nations. He parts seas. He walks on water. He raises the dead. He wins battles. He calms storms. He saves people from sin. He numbers the hairs on our head. He sustains life. He keeps His promises.

The greatness of the Creator-God knows no bounds. He is infinitely powerful. This truth is written on the pages of our heart. It's written on the pages of the night sky.

> I know that thou canst do every thing, and that no thought [no purpose] can be withholden from thee.—Job 42:2

A Purpose in the Pain

So What Have We Learned?

- Believers will suffer—some more than others. But it's destined to happen. It's just part of what it means to be a Christian.

- The ultimate source of our suffering is the decree of God. Satan and nature are simply secondary causes that God uses for His eternal purposes. God is not ashamed for us to know this.

- God is infinitely good. He is love. Nothing ever happens to one of His children that isn't the best possible thing. He works all things together for good to them that love Him.

- God is infinitely powerful. He controls all things. He does whatever He pleases. He can stop bad things from happening if He wants to. There is nothing beyond the scope of His might. He is completely sovereign.

Still No Answers?

If you've followed along thus far, you'll note that we still haven't dealt with the original question that spawned these pages of discussion. It was the question of "why?" Why does God decree for His children to suffer, in some cases intensely? How do we make sense of the martyrdom of John the Baptist or Dave Yarwood or Graham Staines? How do we make sense of cancer, car wrecks, and catastrophe?

As mentioned earlier, we must recognize that when we come to this area we are treading right on the outskirts of an eternal mystery. We cannot expect to piece together perfectly the infinitely wise mind of God. We are limited in our understanding to what our finite minds can comprehend. Yet God has not left us without hope. There *are* answers. It is a glorious discovery that as you search the Scriptures you begin to see the beauty of God's purposes for our pain.

Christlikeness

When a person is born again, he becomes a child of God. God then pursues him the rest of his life to achieve one goal: Christlikeness. Romans 8:29 states, "For whom he did foreknow, he also did predestinate to be conformed to the image of his Son." This process is called *sanctification,* and it doesn't happen overnight. It takes a lifetime.

You see, though we are saved, we still have many, many rough edges to our lives that need to be chiseled away. Our pride is still manifest. Our faith is still "me-centered." Our motives and desires are still tainted with sin. God brings suffering into our lives as a means of chipping away all the rough spots that shouldn't be there. It's a means of helping us along in our sanctification. It's a means of making us look more and more like Christ.

God is a master sculptor who wants the end product to be as beautiful as His own Son. So He picks up the chisel (of suffering) and begins to strike us. The pain is real, and sometimes the suffering seems unbearable. But we know that each blow is guided by

MASTER the TERMS

• *Sanctification:* the process by which the believer becomes less like the old man and more like Jesus Christ

hands of infinite love and skill. He knows just where to strike, and just how much chiseling we can endure at one time. One man has said that "suffering teaches us that the greatest good of the Christian life is not the absence of pain but Christ-likeness."[18] The hurt we experience is not God's ultimate concern—the molding of a pure faith is. Pain is like a mirror that makes us come to terms with the ugliness of our sin. It causes us to despise it and long for more of God's holiness.

Peter stated it this way,

> Wherein ye greatly rejoice, though now for a season, if need be, ye are in heaviness through manifold temptations [trials]: That the trial [genuineness] of your faith, being much more precious than gold that perisheth, though it be tried with fire, might be found unto praise and honour and glory at the appearing of Jesus Christ.—I Peter 1:6-7

A piece of gold on the ground doesn't have nearly the value of a piece of gold that has been refined. But to be refined, gold must pass through very hot fires. The fires are so hot that they almost seem to destroy the gold. Yet what actually happens is that all the impurities in that gold are burned away. The final product? A beautiful piece of precious metal.

Peter says that this is how suffering and persecution function in the life of the believer. They are the "fire" that tries our faith. Notice how Peter describes these trials:

- Their duration is only "for a season"; that is, if you benchmark them against eternity, they do not last a very long time (even if they should last your *whole life* here on earth).

- They occur only "if need be"; that is, if God wills them as necessary in your life. Remember, He is the "who" behind your trials.

- They are "manifold"; that is, there are various types of suffering that you may have to endure. Some are intense, some are not. Furthermore, you might not suffer in the exact same way as another believer.

What then is the net result of all this fire of suffering? It's a faith that is more precious than purified gold! It's a faith that results in "praise and honour and glory at the appearing of Jesus Christ." It's a sanctified life that brightly reflects the image and glory of Christ.

> And not only so, but we glory in tribulations also: knowing that tribulation worketh patience; and patience, experience; and experience, hope.—Romans 5:3-4

> My brethren, count it all joy when ye fall into divers temptations; knowing this, that the trying of your faith worketh patience.
> —James 1:2-3

All of our trials and sufferings are designed "to work" Christlike character down into the fiber of our souls. He desires this so much that He will allow even the worst of disasters to

The hurt we experience is not God's ultimate concern—the molding of a pure faith is.

overtake believers so that the net result will be a precious faith that brings glory to Christ. It has well been said, "God permits what He hates to achieve what He loves."[19] The great plan of God for our lives is that we be conformed to the image of Christ through suffering. Knowing this helps us make sense out of our sorrows.

"Unto the Furtherance of the Gospel"

> "I find that it pleases God to have his truth defended, not by our sword, but by our blood."
> —Earl of Rugenia, upon his execution for following Christ

As you study the Scriptures, one of the things you will discover is that God wills for His kingdom to be expanded through the suffering of the Church. History has proven time and time again that the Church is most effective when it is most persecuted. The testimony of a believer suffering joyfully has a powerful effect upon those who see it.

Martyrdom Modeled

The suffering of a believer is oftentimes used by God as a direct means of communicating the gospel to those who need it. Consider this amazing verse penned by the apostle Paul to the church at Colossae:

> Who now rejoice in my sufferings for you, and fill up [complete] that which is behind [lacking] of the afflictions of Christ in my flesh for his body's sake, which is the church.—Colossians 1:24

Paul is saying that he rejoices in all the suffering he has endured in his body (see II Cor. 11:24-27) because those sufferings "complete" what is "lacking" in Christ's afflictions. Now what could *possibly* be lacking in the sufferings of Christ? Certainly Paul does not mean that anything is lacking in their worth or atoning value. This is made clear from other Scriptures (see Heb.9:12, 10:14, Rom. 5:9).

So what then does Paul mean when he says that his suffering fills up what is lacking in the afflictions of Christ? He simply means this: the sinner lacks the reality of seeing Christ's afflictions. It is no longer possible for lost people to see visibly the sufferings of Christ. Christ does not come down and personally make appearances to the unsaved. He doesn't show them the scars in His hands and feet and side. It is not possible for them to see the agony He suffered—the scourging, the beatings, the thorns, the Cross. In this sense the reality of Christ's sufferings are incomplete. But when a believer suffers for being a Christian before lost people, he makes up for that lack. The Christian becomes a sort of living picture of what the suffering of Christ accomplished for the sinner. When our blood is spilt, it is a living testimony to the Savior whose blood was also spilt. That's why Paul says in Galatians 6:17, "From henceforth let no man trouble me: for I bear in my body the marks of the Lord Jesus." And in II Corinthians 4:10-12 he says,

> Always bearing about in the body the dying of the Lord Jesus, that the life also of Jesus might be made manifest in our body. For we which live are alway delivered unto death for Jesus' sake, that the life also of Jesus might be made manifest in our mortal flesh. So then death worketh in us, but life in you.

Our suffering modeled before a lost world is actually a God-ordained means of furthering the gospel message. In seeing you and me suffer, the sinner actually sees a picture of the suffering Savior.

The Power of Example

Not only does our suffering advance God's kingdom *directly* through confronting and convicting the lost world around us, but suffering is also a powerful means of motivating *other believers* to live white-hot for Jesus and take risks for the kingdom. Paul told the Philippians,

> But I would ye should understand, brethren, that the things which happened unto me have fallen out rather unto the furtherance of the gospel; So that my bonds in Christ are manifest in all the palace, and in all other places; And many of the brethren in the Lord, waxing confident [made bold] by my bonds, are much more bold

to speak the word without fear.—Philippians 1:12-14

Note what Paul says: All of the pain and suffering he experienced for preaching Christ actually resulted in the advancement of the gospel. How so? Well, word of Paul's imprisonment for Christ spread through the whole

> *Our suffering modeled before a lost world is actually a God-ordained means for furthering the gospel message.*

Praetorian guard and to others beyond. What was the result? The other believers saw this and became more courageous to speak the word of God without fear. Paul's bonds ended up giving other believers more boldness!

And that's one of the goals of this book! Our prayer is that as you read the accounts sprinkled throughout this book, God's Spirit would move mightily on your heart and inspire you to imitate the zeal of those who have suffered well and made a difference for the sake of Christ. May their dying testimony make you bold for the kingdom. May you be "followers of them who through faith and patience inherit the promises" (Heb. 6:12).

The Greatness of God's Worth

A lady traveled to the country of Ghana in west Africa. She and her mission group were ministering to disabled believers who lived on the streets of the capital city, Accra. Many of these African Christians had been crippled by polio and were forced to wander the streets as homeless beggars.

One night the missionary lady had the opportunity to attend one of the church services held by these homeless, hurting people. They couldn't meet in the daytime, so they had their church services at night, way down a secluded street. It was on this night that the missionary was introduced to an African named Ama.

Ama had unusable legs, no hands, no bed, and lived in a dilapidated lean-to in a back alley. She combed the streets and picked

The suffering of one Christian can alter the course of a nation. In the following account, note how each man was made bold by his predecessor's example of suffering.

Patrick Hamilton was a young Scottish believer who, in 1520, traveled to the University of Paris to attend college. It was during this time that the great Reformer Martin Luther was turning Europe upside down through his writings and treatises. Eventually Luther's influence and theology came to France, and all the scholars at the University were debating whether it was right or wrong. Patrick was thoroughly caught up in the midst of all this and soon was seized with the truths of the gospel in a new and abiding way.

A short time later Patrick returned to St. Andrews, Scotland to do postgraduate work. Here he was allowed to teach freely and passionately the doctrines of grace and the gospel, much to the dislike of the religious establishment. It was not long before Patrick was tried and condemned for heresy. Within hours he was taken to the stake. Patrick Hamilton—first martyr of the Scottish Reformation, a husband, and father-to-be—was burned to death at St. Andrews in 1528. He was only 23.

It was said after his death that "the reek of good Master Hamilton's death infected all upon whom it blew." One man upon whom it blew was a young schoolteacher named George Wishart. Inspired by the power of the example of Hamilton, Wishart continued the Reformation in Scotland by preaching the gospel and boldly defending the truths of Scripture. In 1546 he too was burned at the stake within yards of the place where Patrick Hamilton was burned.

However, George Wishart had a young man who served as his personal bodyguard. This young man actually carried Wishart's sword. His name was John Knox. After Wishart's death God sent into Knox's soul "the Spirit of God to ordinary men in extraordinary power." Knox soon became the Father of the Scottish Reformation, and by the end of his life, the knowledge of the Lord Jesus Christ was running freely throughout Scotland.

---

through the trash heaps for her meals. She slept on a mattress of hard dirt and broken concrete. Yet Ama was a joy-filled believer. The missionary lady noted that at the midnight church service Ama sang and clapped her arms with a happy enthusiasm as she worshiped her Lord. Her bright smile all but lit up the night.

The missionary was amazed that Ama could have so much joy amidst so much suffering. When asked about it, Ama's response was as stunningly powerful as it was simple. She said, "God is always bigger to those who need Him most."[20]

A final purpose for the pain of believers is seen clearly in these words from Ama. She understood the fact that suffering forces the be-

Suffering forces us to need God.

liever to see God as supremely valuable. As a matter of fact, the worth of God is always seen in what we gladly suffer to gain Him. Suffering pulls out from under us the worldly supports we so often lean on instead of leaning on Him. Suffering forces us to totally rely on God for strength, sustenance, and satisfaction. Suffering causes us to cease finding contentment in self and the world and presses us close to the heart of God. Paul said,

> For we would not, brethren, have you ignorant of our trouble which came to us in Asia, that we were pressed out of measure, above strength, insomuch that we despaired even of life: But we had the sentence of death in ourselves, that we should not trust in ourselves, but in God which raiseth the dead:—II Corinthians 1:8-9

> But we have this treasure in earthen vessels, that the excellency of the power may be of God, and not of us. —II Corinthians 4:7

> And he [the Lord] said unto me, My grace is sufficient for thee: for my strength is made perfect in weakness. Most gladly therefore will I rather glory in my infirmities, that the power of Christ may rest upon me. Therefore I take pleasure in infirmities, in reproaches, in necessities, in persecutions, in distresses for Christ's sake: for when I am weak, then am I strong.—II Corinthians 12:9-10

God's power (or as Ama said, God's "bigness") is shown to be a wonderful thing when we suffer as believers. God goes from being "nice" to becoming an absolute "necessity." *He* becomes the Sustainer of our life. *He* becomes the Provider of our needs. *He* becomes the Comforter of our souls. *He* becomes the Hope of our hearts. And when *God* takes center stage in our lives by becoming our all-satisfying Healer, *God* receives all the glory.

That's why Ama is filled with such overflowing joy even though she is a severely crippled beggar. That's why Paul can "take pleasure" in all his sufferings as a missionary. Though they are weak, and though they are in so much pain, and though life's problems don't always seem to make sense—it really doesn't matter! Because it's then that the "excellency of the power" of an infinitely glorious God is resting upon them and radiating through their lives. That's what makes it worth it all.

Suffering forces us to *need* God. And when we need Him, we learn to rely on Him. And when we rely on Him, we discover His lovingkindness is better than life (Ps. 63:3). And when we abandon ourselves to His care (suffering and all), He receives tremendous glory. Job summed it up well when he said, "Though he slay me, yet will I trust in him" (Job 13:15). For this to be true, God must be the most beautiful, most valuable, most precious, most desirable, most faithful, and most soul-satisfying Being in all the universe.

The truth that God brings suffering into our lives to magnify the power and sufficiency of *Himself* gives meaning to the madness of our trials. And if the supremacy of God's glory is seen most clearly in our joyful response to

personal pain, we are now empowered to view persecution not as an enemy to be avoided, but as a gracious gift to be received and a faithful friend to be embraced.

Conclusion

A Chance to Suffer

Having come to the end of our study together, you may wonder if there are any scriptural examples of the kind of God-centered perspective on suffering that we have presented in this book. Does the Bible actually give real examples of people who embraced suffering as a means of glorifying God? There are many. Such real-life biblical illustrations aid in giving us the hope and courage we need to live and die as we should (Rom. 15:4). Let's consider briefly two examples.

> *Wherefore let them that suffer according to the will of God commit the keeping of their souls to him in well doing, as unto a faithful Creator.—I Peter 4:19*

Taking and Knowing

In Hebrews 10, we read of some Christians who demonstrated a God-centered perspective on life by aiding needy believers even though they knew it might cost them. In verses 32 through 34, we learn that there were believers who were in prison on account of their faith in Christ. Prisons in those days were not designed with the comfort of prisoners in mind. They were usually very dark and damp and used as hideouts for rats and other vermin. Prisoners were given very little, if any, food for survival. So if the prisoners were to survive and not starve to death, food had to come from friends and family.

Bringing food to prisoners created problems especially if they were in prison for religious reasons. If you brought food to a prisoner who was imprisoned for his faith in Christ, you were essentially identifying yourself with the prisoner's religious beliefs. This meant that you were opening yourself up to persecution.

But this very real possibility of persecution did not keep these believers from having compassion upon their suffering brethren (10:34). So what happened to them? They showed compassion on the prisoners, and as a result, experienced the plundering of their goods (10:34). We do not know for sure if this plundering meant that their goods were officially confiscated or thrown out in the streets by an angry mob. In either case they suffered earthly loss.

Verse 34 makes an amazing statement concerning the inner state of these believers when they learned of their loss. It says that they "*took joyfully* the spoiling" of their goods. This is not a normal human response to earthly loss. We are all born spring-loaded to live for the accumulation of earthly things. Most people take great pride in what they own. Yet these believers took the plundering of their goods joyfully. How were they able to respond in this way?

The last half of verse 34 tells us. They responded in this way *knowing* that they had "in heaven a better and an enduring substance." What verse 34 teaches is that these believers were able to take joyfully the loss of their earthly possessions *because* of what they knew they possessed in heaven—"a better and enduring substance." They were believers who could say along with the Apostle Paul that "to live is Christ, and to die is gain." To them there was more joy and more satisfaction to be found in Christ than there was to be found in this world. Having a God-centered orientation on life like this frees you to live godly in this world no matter the cost.

Choosing and Esteeming

From the world's perspective, Moses made some foolish decisions. He had wealth, prestige, and power before him for the taking. Being "called the son of Pharaoh's daughter" (Heb. 11:24) destined him for a life of earthly greatness and ease. But this life of earthly pleasure was not what his heart treasured. Notice the "hard" decisions Moses made in Hebrews 11:24-27. He "refused to be called the son of Pharaoh's daughter; *choosing* rather to suffer affliction with the people of God" (11:24-25a). Refusing to be called the son of Pharaoh's daughter was no small choice. The end of verse 25 tells us that there were pleasures to be enjoyed as a result of having this relationship to Pharaoh. We find in verse 27 that Moses also "forsook Egypt, not fearing the wrath of the king."

How was Moses able to make these "hard" choices? Verse 26 states that he refused sinful pleasures and chose suffering because he considered [esteemed] "the reproach of Christ greater riches than the treasures in Egypt." Egypt offered Moses pleasure, but they were fleeting pleasures (11:25). Moses was not going to give his life away for cheap, two-bit pleasures. He wanted greater riches and lasting pleasures, which this world could not offer. Verse 26 teaches that Moses was able to make these decisions because "he had respect unto the recompence of the reward." In other words, Moses was able to refuse the enjoyment of the fleeting pleasures of sin because he was looking to God as the great rewarder (Heb. 11:6). Moses was looking for superior riches and

pleasures that could be found only in God. Hebrews 11:6 teaches that this kind of looking pleases God. To Moses, to live was Christ even if it meant suffering reproach. Christ was his gain. Moses conquered fear by living for Him [God] who is invisible (11:27). Moses' God-centered orientation on life and death freed him to live godly in the world.

A Hope to Live By

We cannot know what specific plans the Lord may have for your life. But we do know that there will be times that you will suffer for His sake. For some of you it might be the stinging ridicule of a family member or the loss of a job. For others it might be the hostile threatenings of a tribal people or the loss of your life. But whether your suffering is great or small, there is profound, hope-giving comfort in knowing that no matter what comes your way, you are safe in Christ. "For whether we live, we live unto the Lord; and whether we die, we die unto the Lord: whether we live therefore, or die, *we are the Lord's*" (Rom. 14:8). If you are "the Lord's," then no threat of men, no hard circumstance, not even death itself can separate you from Him. Consider these hope-giving words from the apostle Paul found in Romans 8:35-39:

> Who shall separate us from the love of Christ? shall tribulation, or distress, or persecution, or famine, or nakedness, or peril, or sword? As it is written, For thy sake we are killed all the day long; we are accounted as sheep for

the slaughter. Nay, in all these things we are more than conquerors through him that loved us. For I am persuaded, that neither death, nor life, nor angels, nor principalities, nor powers, nor things present, nor things to come, nor height, nor depth, nor any other creature, shall be able to separate us from the love of God, which is in Christ Jesus our Lord.

Jesus told us in Matthew 6:34, "Take therefore no thought for the morrow: for the morrow shall take thought for the things of itself. Sufficient unto the day is the evil thereof." From this verse we learn that every day has its own adversity and therefore future suffering is certain. Perhaps, as you've read this book, you have found yourself becoming fearful of what God may require of you in the future. Perhaps you've wondered if your faith would triumph in the day of tribulation. Yet in this verse, Christ commands us *not* to worry or become anxious about the future. How do we do this?

The answer is found back in the book of Lamentations, a book that contains the greatest cry of a suffering heart in all the Bible. Notice the hope-giving encouragement found in 3:22-23, "It is of the Lord's mercies that we are not consumed, because his compassions fail not. They are new every morning: great is thy faithfulness." Though Christ promises adversity for each day, He also promises us His unfailing lovingkindness *every day;* the same lovingkindness that the Psalmist says "is better than life" (Ps. 63:3).

So what's the point of Matthew 6:34 and Lamentations 3:22-23? It is this: Don't be fearful of the future. The Lord would have us fight tomorrow's pain with tomorrow's grace. Rather than becoming anxious or worried when we consider our future, we can rest assured that the grace we need to make it will be there in the day of adversity. And when the reality of this truth penetrates the depths of our hearts, faith is increased and fear of the future is banished.

So What About You?

Are you willing to commit your life into the hands of God, as unto a faithful Creator (I Pet. 4:19)? Are you willing to turn your back on the two-bit pleasures and comforts of this life and embrace the pleasures of God that last forever (Ps. 16:11)? Are you willing to seek first the kingdom of God, knowing that it is the Father's good pleasure to give it to you (Luke 12:32)?

Our prayer is that the truths contained in this book will motivate you to passionately pursue God. We pray that as your heart is overwhelmed by His infinite goodness and His infinite power, you will gladly go and suffer for His sake. We pray that your faith will be fueled as you daily feast on the gospel. We pray that the Great Rewarder will remove all fear from your heart and empower you to risk everything for the sake of the kingdom. We pray that your life might be a living legacy to the triumphant power of a God-centered faith.

May God ever be your treasure and your joy.

> Weeping may endure for a night, but joy cometh in the morning.—Psalm 30:5

End Notes

[1]Hefley, James C. *By Their Blood.* Milford, MI: Mott Media, 1979, 605-608.

[2]Schlossberg, Herbert. *Called to Suffer, Called to Triumph.* Portland: Multnomah Press, 1990, 9-10.

[3]Hefley, James C. *By Their Blood.* Milford, MI: Mott Media, 1979, 608-609. Porterfield, Bruce. *Commandos For Christ.* Evanston, NY: Harper & Row, 1963, 96-146.

[4]Hendrickson, Ford. *Martyrs and Witnesses.* Detroit: Protestant Missionary Publishing Company, 1917.

[5]Hefley, James C. *By Their Blood.* Milford, MI: Mott Media, 1979, 56-59.

Tucker, Ruth. *From Jerusalem to Irian Jaya.* Grand Rapids: Zondervan, 1983, 421-424.

[6]"The Murder of a Father and His Two Sons." *The Banner of Truth Trust* 1999. 4 April 2001 www.banneroftruth.co.uk//articles/murders.htm.

[7]Ibid.

[8]Mangalwadi, Vishal et al. *Burnt Alive.* Mumbai, India: GLS Press, revised edition, October 1999.

[9]"An Interview with Missionary Gladys Staines." *The Christian Broadcasting Network* 14 Oct 1999. 18 Oct 2000 www.cbn.org/newsstand/cwn/991014c.asp.

[10]As derived from an informal radio transmission, this transcript does not follow the same standards for grammar and punctuation expected in a published work.

[11]Heimbach, Mertis B. *At Any Cost: The Story of Graham Roy Orpin.* London: Overseas Missionary Fellowship, 1964. (Some material taken from the correspondence of Don Rulison and Gillian Orpin; May-June, 1962.)

[12]Organization drawn from Piper, John. "Counting It All Joy." Ligonier Conference. Orlando, FL 2000.

[13]The exegetical insight for this section was received from the following source: Piper, John. *Let the Nations Be Glad.* Grand Rapids: Baker Books, 1993, pp.88-89.

[14]For a further understanding of this concept see Edwards, Jonathan. *The Works of Jonathan Edwards, Vol. 2.* Edinburgh: The Banner of Truth Trust, 1974, p. 902.

[15]Purves, Jock. *Fair Sunshine.* Edinburgh: The Banner of Truth Trust, 1990, 55-62.

[16]The following two sermons by A.N. Martin were very helpful in under-standing the meaning of Phil.1:21: (1) *For to Me to Live is Christ, Phil. 1:21a,* (2) *And to Die is Gain, Phil. 1:21b.* Montville, NJ: Trinity Baptist Church. Audiocassettes. www.tbcnj.org.

[17]Erickson, Millard J. *Christian Theology.* Grand Rapids: Baker Book House, 1983, pp. 283-297.

[18]Tada, Joni Eareckson, and Steve Estes. *When God Weeps.* Grand Rapids: Zondervan, 1997, p. 234.

[19]Tada, Joni Eareckson, and Steve Estes. *When God Weeps.* Grand Rapids: Zondervan, 1997, p. 84.

[20]Tada, Joni Eareckson. "A Bruised Reed." Ligonier Conference. Orlando, FL. 2000.

Photograph Credits

The following agencies and individuals have furnished materials to meet the photographic needs of this textbook. We wish to express our gratitude to them for their important contribution.

International Christian Concern
NASA
New Tribes Mission
Pete Steveson
www.arttoday.com

Introduction
New Tribes Mission, vi

Chapter 1
New Tribes Mission, 1

Chapter 2
www.arttoday.com, 13, 18
Pete Steveson, 20
International Christian Concern, 24

Chapter 5
www.arttoday.com, 68, 70
NASA, 69

Chapter 6
www.arttoday.com, 84-85

Chapter 7
NASA, 91